An Analytical Interpretation of Martin Buber's

I and Thou

MARTIN BUBER

An Analytical Interpretation of Martin Buber's

I and Thou

with a biographical introduction and glossary
by Alexander S. Kohanski

Professor
Department of Philosophy
Kean College of New Jersey

Barron's Educational Series, Woodbury, New York

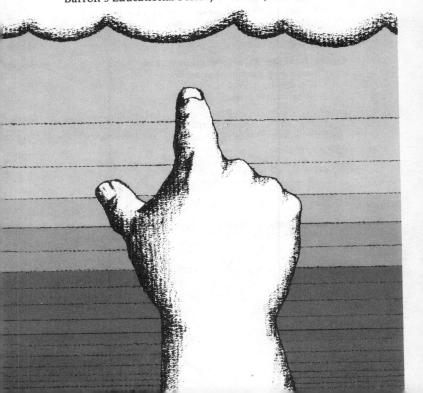

Acknowledgment   The author is grateful to Mr. Rafael Buber of Haifa, Israel, for granting him permission to use the German text of *Ich und Du* as a basis for this *Analytical Interpretation* and to quote certain sentences in direct translation.

All inquiries should be addressed to:
Barron's Educational Series, Inc.
113 Crossways Park Drive
Woodbury, New York 11797

Library of Congress Catalog Card No. 74–4349
International Standard Book No. 0-8120-0505-8

Library of Congress Cataloging in Publication Data
Kohanski, Alexander Sissel, 1902-
   An analytical interpretation of Martin Buber's
I and Thou.
   Bibliography p.
   1. Buber, Martin, 1878-1965. Ich und du.
I. Title.
B3213.B83I235   181'.3   74-4349
ISBN 0-8120-0505-8

TO MY SONS

Daniel and Yoram

with whom I have shared
many thoughts expressed in this work

CONTENTS

PREFACE

MARTIN BUBER'S essay *I and Thou* presents c[...] difficulties to the reader who is not familiar witn its author's mode of thinking and manner of expression. Buber wrote this essay, as he did most of his other works, in a poetic-philosophical style, trying to convey both his immediate experience of reality and his discourse about it. More important, this essay, which he published at a turning point in his philosophical career, constitutes the foundation of his world view, on which he later built his philosophical edifice, elaborating, explaining, interpreting, and expanding it, without ever actually bringing it to completion as a finished product. As he said of all his writings, he was only "pointing the way."

My *Analytical Interpretation* of *I and Thou* is designed to help the student and the general reader toward a fuller understanding of its specific philosophical vocabulary and to guide them along the "way" in which Buber tried to lead man out of the crisis of our time. My work is based on the German text *Ich und Du*, published in Buber's collected essays, *Das dialogische Prinzip* (Verlag Lambert Schneider, Heidelberg, 1962). All quotations from this source are given in my own translation. My *Analytical Interpretation* presents the basic ideas of the essay with explanations of terms, phrases, and passages, in accordance with Buber's philosophy as a whole. As a further aid, I have provided at the end of this book a glossary of the terms which appear most frequently in his philosophical works.

The original text has three parts but no titles, subtitles, or section headings. I have supplied these in my analysis according to major concepts and appropriate subdivisions. I have kept the terminology within the limits of Buber's own word coinage, which I have rendered into English as closely to the original as possible, but not in direct translation, except for quotations. The main feature of my *Analytical Interpretation* is that the content is organized in systematic order, showing the development of the dialogic principle in its various ramifications in the philosopher's thought complex as a whole. At the same time, this work is not meant to supplant the text of Buber's essay and should therefore be read in conjunction with it. To facilitate this procedure, I have indicated at each section heading the page numbers to which it corresponds in Walter Kaufmann's new translation of *I and Thou* (Charles Scribner's Sons, New York, 1970). For the benefit of those who may use Ronald Gregor Smith's translation, I have listed also, at the end of my book, the appropriate page references to the latter's second edition (Charles Scribner's Sons, New York, 1958).

I trust that my efforts will serve the reader as an introduction not only to the text of Buber's *I and Thou* but also to his other writings.

ALEXANDER S. KOHANSKI

Passaic, N.J.
February 1972

xii

INTRODUCTION

The Life and
Works of Martin Buber

MARTIN BUBER addresses himself in all his writings to the probem of modern man, who is "shuddering at alienation between the I and the world," unable to communicate freely and openly with his fellowman, standing helplessly before the overwhelming machine of technology, and, what is most disturbing, losing faith in God, man, and the world. Buber does not offer ready-made solutions to these problems, only "pointing the way" towards the "renewal of dialogical immediacy between men," for this, he says, is the only "hope for this hour."[1]

Early Steps in Home Environment

From his early childhood and throughout his life Buber experienced what he later came to designate as "the principle of dialogue." One day, at the age of eleven, when he was spending his summer vacation at his grandfather's estate, he took great delight in stroking his favorite horse. In this act he experienced the immediacy of the animal as an other with whom he en-

*Note on references. All quotations from the German original are given in my own translation. In the footnotes the English sources are cited in parentheses. If I use translations by others, I refer only to the English title. Full details for works cited only by title (those written by Buber) or by author and title are given in the Bibliography.

[1]*Pointing the Way*, p. 228.

tered into the relation of I and Thou. The horse responded by raising its head, flicking an ear, and snorting quietly, signifying approval of its human friend.[2] Buber attained the same kind of awareness when he would look occasionally into the eyes of a cat, whose glance touched his glance and from whom he learned to know "the nature of actuality in all its relations with being."[3] There were also experiences in his younger days which failed to consummate this relationship and which left an indelible impression on him for life, as, for example, an encounter with his estranged mother.

Buber was born on February 8, 1878, into a well-to-do Jewish family in Vienna. Shortly before he reached the age of three years his parents separated, and he was placed with his paternal grandparents in Lemberg, Galicia, then a province of the Austria-Hungarian Empire. The child yearned for his mother and hoped for her return, until one day, about a year later, his elder companion, who had been entrusted by his grandmother to look after him, told him that his mother would "never come back." He remained silent, and for years afterwards he was still unable to find the word that would convey his feelings at the time, until he coined for himself the term *Vergegnung,* meaning "the failure of a real meeting between persons." Years later, after he had become a family man, his mother visited him once, but again there was a *Vergegnung*—no real meeting between them. In real meeting, he came to

[2]*Begegnung. Autobiographische Fragmente,* (Stuttgart: W. Kohlhammer Verlag, 1961), pp. 15-16 (P. A. Schilpp and M. Friedman, eds., *The Philosophy of Martin Buber,* p. 10).
[3]*Ich und Du, Werke* I, pp. 143-144 (*I and Thou.* Kaufmann translation, p. 105).

realize, there is an encounter between mutually independent beings who confirm each other in mutual response and responsibility. The opposite of this is what
he termed *Vergegnung*, which may thus be translated as
a *"misencounter."*[4] We may wonder why Buber was so
much disturbed for a long time by his inability to find
just the right word for this particular experience. To
him, language, the word, meant a primal power expressing reality. The word cannot be spoken except to an
other; it is "man's will to communicate."[5] Speech is
identical with revelation. Buber, like Franz Rosenzweig,
was in search of "the method of the philosophy of language."[6] In essence, this is the path that he followed in
his entire thinking process. He was well prepared for it
in his grandparents' home, where under the influence
of his grandmother he studied several languages and
came to sense their primal origins.

Adele Buber, the grandmother, was self-educated in
world literature, especially German, as it was not the
custom in the small village in Galicia where she grew
up to give girls a formal education. At the age of seventeen she married Solomon Buber, and in the manner of
the time devoted herself to the management of her husband's landholdings and phosphate mines, in order to
allow him more leisure for his Talmudic-Midrashic
studies, in which he excelled as editor and interpreter.
Until the age of ten young Buber received his early
education in Hebraic traditional lore as well as in secu-
lar studies under the loving care of his grandparents at

[4]*Begegnung*, pp. 5–6 (*The Philosophy of Martin Buber*,
pp. 3–4).
[5]*Werke* I, p. 443 (*Knowledge of Man*, p. 111).
[6]*Pointing the Way*, p. 88.

home. As he reminisced later in his *Autobiographical Fragments*, "grandfather was a true philologist, one who 'loves the word,' but grandmother's love for the genuine word exerted greater influence on me than his, because her love was so immediate and so pious."[7] Later he enrolled in the Franz-Joseph Gymnasium, where the language of instruction was Polish, although the general atmosphere of the school was of the Austria-Hungarian Monarchy. In those formative years he came also into contact with the ways of the Hasidim in Sadagora, a small town in the province of Bukowina, where he spent his summer months on his father's nearby estate. Occasionally, his father would take him along on visits to the Sadagorer Rebbé, the well-known head of a Hasidic dynasty. What particularly impressed Buber then was the implicit faith of the Hasidim in the powers of their spiritual leader, or the *zaddik,* as he was called, to help them in all affairs of everyday life on earth. It appeared to his young imagination that what the world needed was the perfect man, for only such a man could be the helper of mankind in mundane as well as in spiritual matters.

At the age of fourteen Buber left his grandparents' home and went to live with his father, who had remarried by then and settled in Lemberg. As he was now able to observe his father's ways more directly, his searching mind tried to find some fundamental element in the latter's relation to reality. His father was a phenomenally successful mine operator and big landowner. But notwithstanding his wealth, broad education, and high standing in the community, he showed a sense

[7]*Begegnung*, p. 8 (*The Philosophy of Martin Buber*, pp. 4–5).

of primary relationship to nature and to fellowman. It was an immediate "genuine human contact with nature—an active and responsible contact." The same immediacy was shown in his relations with all men, whether those of equal social status with him, or the poor and needy, or his subordinates in his business enterprises. His was a relation "through genuine contact" of person to person. His interest in people simply as human beings was always reflected in his conversations about them as he portrayed their lives with the gift of "an elemental story-teller."[8] Perhaps Martin Buber remembered his father most lovingly for having brought him into the presence of the Sadagorer Rebbé. When he published his "Reminiscences" of his way to Hasidism, in 1918, he dedicated the work to his "beloved father."[9]

Encounter with the Outside

Then came Buber's first encounter with two philosophers, Kant and Nietzsche, who influenced greatly his approach to the problems of man. From the former he learned, after reading his *Prolegomena to Any Future Metaphysic* at the age of fifteen, that space and time "are nothing but formal conditions of our sensibility," and "not real qualities inherent in the things." Buber had been deeply vexed by the problem of conceiving time and space equally as limited and limitless in reality. Kant's philosophy had a highly pacifying influence on him, as it assured him that the question was not one

[8]*Ibid.*, pp. 10–11 (*The Philosophy of Martin Buber*, pp. 6–7).

[9]*Mein Weg zum Hassidismus: Erinnerungen*, (Frankfurt a.M., 1918).

of the real state of things-in-themselves, but only of man's way of apprehending them in appearance.

The other philosopher, Nietzsche, whose book *Thus Spoke Zarathustra* also deals with the fundamental meaning of time, had the opposite effect on Buber when he read it at the age of seventeen. The work overwhelmed him, surging against him and threatening to rob him of his freedom. Nietzsche's teaching of "eternal recurrence of the same" appeared to him as the *fatum* of time, an illusive mystery to which man succumbs with relentless necessity. Buber could ask no questions about it, as he was able to do regarding Kant's concept of time. In later years he further noted, "Nietzsche's Zarathustra wanted to enlighten me in my youth that God is dead. But grand as it seemed, that could be recognized as Feuerbach's old confusion of a human idea of God with the real God."[10] Again when he was in his eighties he recalled the "rousing influence" of "Zarathustra," which "carried me off into the realm of sublime intoxication, from which I was able to escape completely only after a long time and get on the road to certainty of the real."[11]

During his school years at the Franz-Joseph Gymnasium Buber shed the traditional Jewish outlook on life and its ritual and observances which he had learned and practiced until his fourteenth year at his grandparents' home. As he began to probe, under the influence of his new surroundings, into the philosophical issues of the time, his earlier enthusiasm for the Hasid-

---

[10]*Der Jude und sein Judentum*, p. 810. *Cf. Israel and the World*: "The Prejudice of Youth," p. 50.

[11]*Begegnung*, p. 16 (*The Philosophy of Martin Buber*, p. 11).

ic way of life waned and he became estranged not only from Hasidism but also from Judaism as a whole.[12] In the student years which followed at the universities of Vienna, Berlin, and Leipzig, he turned to art, literature, music, and philosophy, and was carried away by the esthetic-cultural trend which then prevailed among the youth in the intellectual centers of Germany and Austria. During this period of his life, which lasted until his twentieth year and to some extent even beyond, as he described it later, he was seized by "the whirl of the age." He lived in a "world of confusion, a mythical habitation of roving souls with the fulness of spiritual agility, but without Judaism, and thus without humanity and without the presence of the divine."[13]

Return to the Fold

In the next period, 1898–1904, Buber underwent a spiritual change by freeing himself from the illusory world and striking roots in the realities of the Jewish people, and through them, in the realities of mankind as a whole. His first step was the embracing of Zionism, which marked a basic trend in his mode of thinking: to see the individual as the bearer of the universal or to blend the finite with the infinite. Zionism for him meant not just the establishment of a Jewish state in a given territory, but rather the revival of all the creative forces of the Jewish people, the realization of their ideals, a national cultural movement that transcends party lines and also goes beyond the narrow confines

---

[12]*Werke* I: "Mein Weg zum Hassidismus," p. 965 (*Hasidism and Modern Man*, p. 55).

[13]*Ibid.*, p. 966 (*Hasidism and Modern Man*, p. 57).

of egotistic nationalism, which was then on the rise among Western European nations. Buber saw in Zionism the road to a regenerate Judiasm, the renewal of the Jewish people and the redemption of the individual through the nation as a whole. He saw the problem of the people as the problem that confronts each individual Jew and, therefore, one that is to be resolved through his personal ties with his people. Furthermore, just as the individual is the bearer of the national spirit, so is each nation the bearer of the spirit of humanity.

Buber was active for a few years in the World Zionist Organization, which was founded and led by Theodor Herzl; but having found himself in disagreement with its policies, he withdrew from it after Herzl died, in 1904. However, he remained a Zionist throughout his life in the spirit in which he understood the movement.

In 1899, when Buber was attending the University at Zurich, he met Paula Winkler, a non-Jewess of Munich, who later became his wife, converted to Judaism upon their marriage, and remained his life-long coworker for the Zionist and Jewish causes. While raising Eva and Rafael, their two children, Mrs. Buber also wrote stories which gained prominence for her under her pen-name of Georg Munk. She had great influence on her husband's creative development, as was attested by a poem he wrote on his fiftieth birthday: "You influenced me to look/ Influenced? You just lived/ You element and woman/ Soul and nature!"[14]

Another turn in Buber's life at that time came through

[14]Hans Kohn, *Martin Buber: Sein Werk und seine Zeit*, pp. 25, 291–292.

his association with the movement for the creation of a "New Community" (*Neue Gemeinschaft*), in which he took an active part as member and lecturer. There he met Gustav Landauer, leader of this circle, with whom he formed a close friendship and who influenced his views on the relationship between individual and society. Those were revolutionary days for both these friends, but, contrary to Marxist doctrine, they conceived of a new society arising not through the rule of the proletariat but through an inner change, a "return" of individual man. "We do not want revolution —we are revolution," Buber proclaimed in one of his lectures on the old and new community.[15] He was then also preoccupied with the study of German mysticism from Cusa to Böhme, which was the subject of his doctoral dissertation in 1904. Other influences on his philosophical development at the time came from two of his teachers at the University of Berlin, Georg Simmel and Wilhelm Dilthey. The first led him to look for the infinite in life in the light of finite being, and the second shaped his mode of observing man-as-a-whole, thus laying the foundation for his philosophical anthropology.

In these formative years Buber still remained outside the religious sphere. But as he became active in the Zionist movement he sought also to deepen his knowledge of the sources of Judaism. His adherence to Zionism, as he emphasized later, was only a beginning, a return to the fold of his origin. What he strove after was a transformation (*Verwandlung*) of his inner life. He professed Judaism before he knew it, he said. He

[15]*Ibid.*, p. 29.

then took the second step to gain "the immediate knowing . . . of the people in its creative primal hours."[16]
This led him on the way to Hasidism. He studied the
lore of the Hasidim, observed their inner way of life,
translated the tales of their *zaddikim*, and tried to live
through the primal reality of their everyday relationships. With all that, Buber never really became a Hasid,
nor did he claim ever to be one, for he never returned
to the sacral practices and observances according to
Talmudic law, which have remained a fundamental part
of the life of a Hasid. Although his philosophical world
outlook was moulded by his Hasidic studies and observations, his Hasidism was at best only an interpretation.
He saw in it a genuine representation of the religious
reality of historical Judaism, a genuine return of Jewish-
ness to its primary source, and it was this source, rather
than the actual life of the Hasid that brought about a
transformation in his personal life. He envisioned in
Hasidism the dialogical encounter between man and
God, which he later developed into his philosophy of
I and Thou. His studies of Hasidism were further
deepened during the years 1905–1912 by his research
and writings on the epos and tales of Finland, China,
and other countries, in which he explored the powers
of myth and poetry as expressions of the primary relation between man and God.

Realization in Direction

At the end of this period, early in 1913, Buber published his first major philosophical essay, *Daniel: Conversations about Realization.* It was a culmination of

[16]*Hasidism and Modern Man*, p. 58.

his development in the esthetic-cultural mode of thinking, dominated by Greek thought as it came to him through his teachers at the universities in Vienna and Berlin, and especially through the writings of Nietzsche. There is also evidence in the book of a struggle to free himself of this mode, but he remains anchored in the boundless sea of the artistic creative spirit in which he tries to find the force that binds together. Such a force, Buber discovers, is in man, who, if he wills, can unite within his soul all the contradictions and opposites of the world. To use Nietzsche's description, Buber sees this kind of human being as "a man who constantly experiences extraordinary things, . . . who is himself perhaps a thunderstorm pregnant with new lightnings; a fateful man around whom there is always peeling, growling and yelping, and things go weird. . . ."[17] He is a man of daring who does not shrink from danger but welcomes it, who lives in the realm of eternal becoming, of holy uncertainty.[18]

The theme of *Daniel* is man's craving for unity. But unity is not something to be found; it can be attained only through action by the man who wills it. However, instead of "will to power" Buber posits the will to act through "direction," which propels man to real unity. Following Dilthey's distinction between the natural sciences and cultural science (*Geisteswissenschaft*), Buber draws a more fundamental distinction between what he designates as *orientation* for the former, and *realization* for the latter. These are man's basic approaches to the

[17]Friedrich Nietzsche, *Jenseits von Gut und Böse* (*Beyond Good and Evil*) #292.
[18]*Daniel: Gespräche der Verwirklichung*, (Leipzig: im Insel-Verlag, 1919), p. 77.

world. In the first he wants to be sure of his ground,
observe all the particulars of each thing and event, compare, calculate, and relate them to one another, and
set them up within a coordinate system—in a word,
follow the scientific way of orienting oneself in the
world of things. This gives man a sense of security; he
can always find the exact place for everything around
him. But in his innermost being he is not satisfied with
this kind of security, as it gives him only a semblance
of repose and safety against the onslaught of the world
of things: he may know the place of each thing in coordination with other things, but not in their reality.
Real knowledge he can attain only through realization,
that is, through living experiences with things; for a
thing becomes what it is in reality through the unifying
act of man's soul, which experiences it. Reality is thus
the work of the soul, yet is produced by the soul not
like an object for observation and classification, but as
a living experience, incomprehensible like lightning or
a waterfall. Such is the dynamics of the things of the
world as lived by man every moment that he acts with
his being as a whole, creating a unity. This creative act
is propelled by what Buber designates as man's "inborn
direction." It is the force that chooses a particular unit
out of endless possibilities and renders it actual. "Direction is that primal tension of the human soul which
moves it at times out of the infinity of the possible to
choose this and nothing else and to realize it through
action."[19]

Now what exactly is the nature of this directional action? At this point Buber rejects his earlier view that
a state of ecstasy may bring man into unity with the

[19]*Ibid.*, pp. 18–19.

world of things. What he advocates now is not unification of the knower *with* the known, but the unifying of the known as such through the unification of the knower *in* himself. Neither does he teach absorption of the knower into the known through a mystic elimination of all differences between them, but suggests an ingathering of all the possibilities of the thing within man's soul, as if they were his own possibilities, and a binding of them together in one reality. This is what Buber calls the act of realization. In it the soul's forces of direction choose the possibilities which are to become actual. Thus not blind necessity but the "directed soul" renders the world of things real and, to that extent, meaningful.

If reality is unity, where do multiplicity and, with it, infinite possibility come from? In his book *Daniel* Buber discusses this question not from an ontological or metaphysical point of view but rather as a problem of epistemology, that is, how we conceive of multiplicity as a unity in reality. In terms of his dynamic of knowledge, the question is, How do we know that unity can be attained? For unity is not a given to be discovered but a state to be realized in the very act of knowing. Buber rests his case on the principle of the Greek mode of thinking, which says, "Only like knows like." Everything in the world is a duality of infinite possibilities, and so is man. It is a duality in the nature of a *polarity*, such as being and not-being, good and evil, or positive and negative. Between them is a stream of tensions, antagonisms, contradictions, oppositions. The meaning of the world is the truth of its duality,[20] and "whoever

[20]*Ibid.*, Third Conversation, p. 80.

experiences the world in truth experiences it as a duality."[21] Man knows the tension of polarity in the world of things through the tension of polarity in his own soul. If he is to attain unity, that is, know the world of things, his primary task is to master the tension, not abolish it, and rather than absorbing one pole into the other, to take his stand in the midst of the stream, where he will become his real self, the *I* which binds the poles into a bipolar unity. In living experience here and now on earth (and this is the only human experience Buber is concerned with) contradictions and opposites do not disappear, nor are they to be considered as illusions. Their unity is realized in the very stream which flows between their poles through man himself, as he becomes the binding force when he decides to act through his "directed soul." This is the moment when man may speak of himself as the *I* who exists in reality and not just as a grammatical subject of general speech. "In truth there is no I except the I of tension."[22] The greater the tension we take upon ourselves, the greater the I in us. "The high test of our existence is to live world-tension."[23]

There are many elements in the philosophy of *Daniel* which later came to fruition in the essay *I and Thou*. Such are the primary view of the world as "here and now" and not as "here and hereafter," the *between* (the stream between the poles) as the reality in which man must take his stand, *direction* which leads to reality, *freedom* which is in man's own destiny to act with direction, and, especially, the emphasis on immediate

[21]*Ibid.*, Fifth Conversation, p. 139.
[22]*Ibid.*, p. 149.
[23]*Ibid.*, p. 150.

living experience (*Erlebnis*) as distinguished from mediated experience (*Erfahrung*) of objects for observation and use. However, man here is still conceived as a dual being who is to realize himself as an *I* within himself, not in relation to another, a *Thou*. He is to embrace the duality of things and unite it within his own duality, like a lintel over the two poles of polarity. The goal for the greatest I is the unity of the world. "This I is the I of the world. In it the unity fulfills itself."[24] Although God is mentioned a few times in *Daniel*, it is only to express His domain in which the greatest binding force may exercise itself, but not to indicate the Being that man encounters as the Absolute Thou.[25]

The most important aspect of the book *Daniel* is that it presents the fundamental problem of modern man who is dominated by the spirit of science and technology and cannot find his way to reality. As in his later works, here too Buber does not advocate the elimination of scientific and technological advancements but rather their subordination to the forces of living experience. Man, he says, cannot live by "orientation" alone or by "realization" alone. What has brought about the present crisis is that orientation reigns supreme with overwhelming power. Only the men who may become aware of their forces of "inborn direction" will counteract this trend and lead man out of his crisis. This is the theme of all of Buber's subsequent writings; it found its fullest expression in his work *I and Thou*.

[24]*Ibid.*, p. 151.
[25]*Ibid.*, Third Conversation, pp. 70–71. "God cannot realize himself to man except as the innermost present of living experience. . . ."

Years of Decision—Relating and Distancing

Buber came to consider the years 1916–1920 as a period of decision in the development of his entire thought-complex.[26] It was during that time that his mode of thinking crystallyzed into a religious world outlook which assumed an ontological character and found expression in the word-formation of his basic essay *I and Thou*, issued in 1923. In a Postscript some forty years later he recalled that when he drafted the first sketch of this book he was driven by an inner necessity, by an insight which had troubled him since his youth, often dimmed and then clarified again, until it became so clearly suprapersonal that he felt he had to bring it to the attention of others.[27] Its burden is man's ontic capacity to communicate with fellowman, nature, and divine being without mediation. The relation is one of mutuality, but without subordination of one to the other and without the identification or fusion of any. Each is a being exclusive of the other, yet the relation represents an inclusion of all that one may have experienced prior to each particular encounter with the other. This act manifests itself in four potencies: cognition, art, love, and faith, the last being the greatest and embracing them all. It is faith which places man in relation to God, or it is that which occurs *between* man and God when the former goes out with his being-as-a-whole to meet the Divine Being. The meeting between man and God, as well as between man and man, and man and nature, is called the I-Thou relation. How-

[26]*Cf. Werke* II, p. 1175.
[27]*Cf. Werke* I, p. 161 (*I and Thou*, p. 171).

ever, man does not, nay cannot, remain in this state
of immediacy for more than moments at a time. When
he steps out of it, he sees the other as a thing of use,
enjoyment, calculation, classification, and scientific observation, as an It. More correctly, man is then in a
state of I-It connection or mediated experience.

This dual way of communication, the first of entering-
in-relation with another, and the second of distancing
from him, Buber considers to constitute the two primal
characteristics of man, his category of being human.
". . . To be man means to be *the* being that is over
against."[28] This trait manifests itself in speech, which,
too, is an exclusively human capacity: "Man, he alone,
speaks, because only he can address the other even as
another who stands at a distance opposite him; but as
he addresses it, he enters-into-relation. The coming-
to-be of language, though, also signifies a new function of distance."[29] That is, in speech man may express
his mediated experience only insofar as it originated
in immediacy.

In the light of this view of man in relation to the
world, fellowman, and God, the meaning of human
existence, which has become the most troublesome problem of our time, assumes a different aspect. "The fundamental fact of human existence," says Buber, "is man
with man."[30] The problem now is centered not on man
as "the single one" in himself alone, or on man in the
aggregate, but on what occurs between them. The crisis
of the modern age, as Buber views it, is thus "the crisis

[28]P. A. Schilpp and M. Friedman, eds., *The Philosophy
of Martin Buber*, p. 35, Appendix II.
[29]*Werke* I, p. 449 (*Knowledge of Man*, p. 117).
[30]*Between Man and Man*, p. 203.

of the between," which is of a threefold nature. It is the crisis in human freedom as a scientific issue of relating man to the rest of nature; the crisis in interhuman relations as a technological issue of the media of production and communication; and the crisis in religion as the theological issue of relating man to God. These three issues correspond in general to the three parts of the book *I and Thou.* Everything Buber wrote and taught afterwards emanates directly or indirectly from this book. In his own words, " 'I and Thou' stands at the beginning [of the dialogic principle], everything else is only illustration and completion."[31]

The Life of Faith

Buber found the power of the Word expressed most potently in the Bible. "The Hebrew Bible," he thought, "is essentially formed and articulated through the language of the message," that is, the spoken word.[32] For a long time he had harbored the idea of translating the Hebrew text into German in keeping with this spirit of spokenness. In this connection his friendship with Franz Rosenzweig bore the greatest fruit. In 1925 he succeeded in convincing Rosenzweig to join him in this enterprise, and during the next four years, until the latter's death in 1929, they translated Genesis through Isaiah. Thereafter Buber continued the work by himself, completing it in 1961.

As he worked on the translation he delved into the exegesis of the Bible, its historical background and the meaning of its message to man in all epochs. His writ-

[31]*Cf. Dialogisches Leben*: Vorwort. Quoted by Robert Weltsch in Hans Kohn's *Martin Buber, op. cit.,* p. 454.
[32]*Werke* II, p. 1095.

ings on the subject reflect the maturity of his mode of thinking and, in turn, are reflected in his other works on philosophy, the social sciences, and education. In his Introduction to the volume *Schriften zur Bibel* (*Werke* II) he points to the fact that his Biblical essays were written almost two decades after he had published his main works on philosophy and Hasidism. "This tells me," he said, "that I had first to mature in service of the Bible."[33] This, he further noted, is true of everyone who has been distanced from it and tries to reach it again in truth.

Buber's Biblical works deal not with a given history of religion but chiefly with a history of faith of a particular people, which reveals the believing potency of man as a whole. By this Buber means that he is not discussing the "religious teachings, religious symbols and religious practices as such," which are the customary subject-matter of theology and religious institutions. Instead, he deals with faith as such, as of "the common life-relations of a community" shaped in "all its social, political, and spiritual functions" through the immediate relation of that community with God as its King and Ruler.[34] This relation of man with God, as said earlier, *is* faith. Buber found in the Jewish Bible the authentic record of the I-Thou experience of which man is capable, the kind of experience which taxes his highest potency of acting as a human being-as-a-whole, and which is manifest in the spoken word. This is revealed particularly in the person of the prophet. One of Buber's

[33]*Cf. Der Jude and sein Judentum*, p. 141, on Buber's advice to youth to read the Bible "as a service of knowing (*aus dienendem Wissen*) the soul of the primal Hebrew language, but not as a work of literature. . . ."

[34]*Moses*, p. 9. *Cf. The Prophetic Faith*, p. 7.

aims, therefore, was to establish the Biblical sources which show the primacy of man's unity as a being who enters into relation with the Absolute Thou and his subsequent dualization into "relating" and "distancing," which in essence is the philosophy of *I and Thou*. To be sure, the twofold way of Biblical man's communication with being was inherent in his primal state, but it was kept unified in the same person, namely, the prophet-leader. The duality ensued when the latter divided his functions between the prophet and the priest. This distinction is fundamental to our understanding of Buber's view of the message of the Jewish Bible.

The prophet, says Buber, is "that undivided, entire person who as such receives the message and as such endeavours to establish that message in life."[35] The priest, on the other hand, is a man who holds the specific office of administering sacral rites through traditional "divinary methods" within an established system of prescribed laws. He "is the greatest human specialization that we know." The prophet, on the contrary, is unspecialized. What singles him out "as such" is the way he receives the divine message and, even more so, the way he seeks to carry it into life. Both ways are of the "spirit of the word," in contrast to the "spirit of force." Here again Buber places the power of the word, as the living experience of "a dialogic relationship with the Divinity," above the power of ecstasy, which takes possession of man as "an impersonal, wordless force."[36]

[35]*Ibid.*, p. 200.

[36]*Ibid.*, pp. 164–166. The contrast is drawn in comparing the spirit of the word, which *is* over Moses repeatedly, with the "wordless spirit" of ecstasy, which "comes to rest" only for a while on the Seventy Elders whom Moses chose to help him bear the burden of the people in the Wilderness.

In the same way, the prophet carries the divine message of the word to the people, not by using temporal force, not by compulsion, but through the spontaneous power of the word itself, by showing the way of "return." The prophet is not a diviner of future redemption. He presents the people with a choice and a decision which may lead to redemption, but the determining factor in shaping the future is the people's decision to return to the ways of God.[37] By "return" Buber means the renewal of everyday life in the spirit of the word, which is manifest in both "divine freedom" and "divine law." There is no contradiction between the two in reality. "God rules through men who have been gripped and filled by His spirit, and who on occasion carry out His will not merely by means of instantaneous decisions but also through lasting justice and law."[38] But it often happens in human affairs that the world of law becomes emptied of the spirit yet continues to claim divine authority. The prophet's *true* admonition to the people, and particularly to its elders and rulers, "is that the law must again and again immerse itself in the consuming and purifying fire of the spirit. . . ."[39] Buber regards this prophetic function to be in the direct line of the "Mosaic principle of ever-recurrent renewal," which is the core of faith exemplified in the Hebrew Bible in general.[40]

The unique quality of the prophetic faith Buber finds originally in Moses, who was "that undivided, entire person," the messenger of God's word, legislator, and

[37]*The Prophetic Faith*, pp. 2–3.
[38]*Moses*, p. 187.
[39]*Ibid.*, p. 188.
[40]*Ibid.*

leader—"the prophetic leader"—whose law giving and law enforcement were always filled with the spirit of the word. In him were united the functions of "the sacral utterance of oracles, the direction of communal offerings, and the political organization and leadership of the people's life. . . ."[41] He was not "merely a combination of priest and prophet," that is, he was not holding two departmental offices. His task was "the realization of the unity of religious and social life in the community of Israel. . . ." This "mingled the elements of his soul into a most rare unity."[42] At the end of his career, when he chose Joshua to take over the leadership, he found it necessary to divide his functions between "judge" and "priest," thus splitting the unity "in the order of the people and, together with that, in every individual soul as well."[43]

This interpretation of the Bible is grounded in Buber's ontology of man's twofold communication with the other as I-Thou and I-It, the first experienced by the entire man, the second by divided man. The priest, when devoid of the spirit of the word, is that divided man who takes his stand in the word-pair I-It and promotes the world of It. It is then incumbent on the prophet, the undivided man, to take his stand in the word-pair I-Thou and to lead the people back to their primal relation with the Eternal Thou.[44] Buber does not mean to signify that there are two types of men, one

[41]*Ibid.*, p. 198.
[42]*Ibid.*, p. 186.
[43]*Ibid.*, p. 199.
[44]*Cf. The Prophetic Faith*, p. 230, on the anonymous prophet Deutero-Isaiah, who may have recognized in himself one of the persons doing the work of redemption of world history.

prophetic and the other priestly, but says that man as such may act in one state or the other, depending on his decision or lack of it, as the case may be, to live according to his "inner direction."[45] In the case of Moses himself, when he acted with a show of force instead of through the word during the Korah rebellion, or when he separated the functions of the priest from those of the prophet in the appointment of Joshua, Buber considers these events as tragic in the life of the prophetic leader. In these acts Moses suffered a division in his own person and a breakdown in the central foundation of his work, which was to carry out the message of Divine revelation through "unified persons." He had to yield to "the resistance of the human material," to the splitting of persons, which "is the historical way of mankind."[46]

In the course of his Biblical studies Buber also devoted considerable attention to the New Testament, not so much as the sacred writings of the Christian religion, but rather as the source of the life and teaching of the person Jesus. In Buber's view there is a cardinal difference between these two aspects. "From my youth onwards," he said, "I have found in Jesus my great brother," and this fraternal relationship grew ever stronger as he studied the New Testament for almost fifty years.[47] As he reviews the history of Israel's faith (but not its history of religion, as indicated above), he finds a place for Jesus in that history as "understood from Israel," though not as "understood from Christianity." "The latter," he says, "I have touched only

[45]*Cf. Moses*, p. 200.
[46]*Ibid.*, pp. 189, 199.
[47]*Two Types of Faith*, p. 12.

with the unbiased respect of one who hears the Word."[48]

Buber maintains that Jesus did not consider himself the divine mediator between man and God but, on the contrary, saw his own relation to God as that of faith according to the Jewish prophetic tradition, that is, in the immediacy of receiving the Divine message and in serving God with the highest intention of carrying that message into life. Furthermore, Jesus did not oppose the Pharisees, in whose midst he grew up and whose true teachings of the Torah he absorbed and preached, as such. But there were among the Pharisees "two-faced" men who tried to congeal the living word of the Torah into fixed legalistic concepts of external observances. It was these men that Jesus opposed and denounced, as they were also denounced by other true Pharisees who sought to uphold and revive the primal character of the Torah as revelation and teaching, that is, in the true prophetic tradition. In Buber's words, "For the actuality of the faith of Biblical and post-Biblical Judaism, and also for the Jesus of the Sermon on the Mount, fulfilment of the Torah means to extend the hearing of the word to the whole dimension of human existence."[49] As for Buber's own creed with regard to the Messiah and world redemption, he once stated it in a letter to a Christian-Jewish association in Hamburg: "According to my belief, God does not reveal Himself in man but only through man. . . . The Messiah did not appear in a definite moment in history, but his appearance can only be the end of history. . . . The redemption of the world did not occur nineteen hundred years ago, but we still live in the unredeemed

[48]*Ibid.*, p. 13.
[49]*Ibid.*, p. 58.

world and await redemption in which every one of us is called upon to participate in an inexplicable manner."[50]

To sum up Buber's philosophy of religion, his vision of redemption is the establishment of the Kingdom of God here and now on earth in every act of the human being-as-a-whole. In this act man is in partnership with God. The meeting of the finite with the infinite is not *in* man but *between* him and the Absolute. Their mutuality is an act of redemption. In this very act, as man returns God redeems.

Dialogue with Youth

Many of the young generation in Western Europe found direction for their aspirations in Buber's writings and especially in his personal talks at student gatherings on various occasions. While he spoke directly to the youth of his own people, his message was of a universal character, touching on the social and religious problems of all peoples, in particular on the role of the individual in relation to his community and to mankind. He had a feeling for youth, for its hunger for experience, its passion for a cause, its vehement defense of the side it has chosen, but also its reluctance to hear the other side for fear that its own position may thereby be put into question. He spoke of what we are now likely to consider as the generation gap, the young people's rebellion against what is old and "established," their rejection of history, and their eagerness to do things by themselves differently and hopefully better.

[50]Quoted in Franz von Hammerstein, *Das Messiasproblem bei Martin Buber* (Stuttgart: W. Kohlhammer, 1958), p. 49.

He saw in this spirit of youth much that is "fine and fruitful," yet warned that it is fraught with danger when prejudice and lack of faith keep young people from seeing the past in the right light and prevent "the living stream of tradition from entering their souls."[51]

He spoke of truth and responsibility, spontaneity, faith, and the images of God. Can one find truth when all is relative? Perhaps not. But one "can have an honest and uncompromising attitude toward truth." It becomes real only through one's life, that is, "the life of personal responsibility." This manifests itself in our personal relationships with fellowman when we do not hold ourselves back but open up spontaneously to one another, in true communality, for without it man cannot realize his humanity.

Buber was mindful of youth's complaint that religious institutions often act in many ways contrary to the truth of faith. But this should not mean that youth must seek a new formula, because real faith is not handed down in formulas. There is an unconditional mystery in every one of our daily actions, and the man of faith holds himself open to the encounter with life "in the face of this mystery," difficult as this may sometimes be. In these experiences we can gain strength from those who have lived with such mystery before us, those who engaged their lives in it, for that is the way of faith—"to engage oneself."

The greatest trial of faith for the youth of today, Buber went on to say, comes when they go out on the way to God and hear leading theologians and philosophers announce that He is dead. Youth must understand the meaning of such a statement. It signifies a

[51]*Israel and the World*: "The Prejudice of Youth," p. 42.

confusion of the real God with images of God which man fashions again and again, only to discover that he cannot make an image of God in reality. Man then can no longer worship the image as God and is bound to break it. Such is the soul of the iconoclast: he cannot bear the existence of an image in which he no longer believes. This is the way of man in all generations. But let youth listen to the voice of God, which is never silenced: "it speaks to the men of all generations, makes demands upon them, and summons them to accept their responsibility. . . . It does not matter what you call it. All that matters is that you hear it."[52]

Education and the Restructuring of Society

In December 1923 Buber was invited by the University of Frankfurt to lecture on the philosophy of Jewish religion. He continued in this post for ten years, and by 1933, when the Nazis came into power, he was honorary professor of comparative philosophy of religion. These were years of intense creativity by himself and in collaboration with his friend Franz Rosenzweig, with whom he was also associated in the *Freies jüdisches Lehrhaus* (a Jewish folk university established in Frankfurt in 1920), of which the latter was the founder and guiding spirit. Both friends were deeply involved in problems of education or, as Rosenzweig conceived it, in the problem of learning as the essence of living. But at the very start of the Nazi regime the winds were already blowing fiercely against all Jewish academicians in the higher seats of learning, which soon

[52]*Ibid.*, p. 51.

came under government control. In the fall of 1933 Buber resigned from the University of Frankfurt without waiting to be dismissed. He then turned his energies to teaching, lecturing, advising, and encouraging the stricken Jewish population in Germany, whose fate had already been sealed, though the Jews themselves were kept unaware of this fact.

Buber's main efforts were directed toward adult Jewish education and to the re-education of young people, most of whom had been estranged from their tradition. He traveled through the towns and cities, where he lectured and taught in the hope of restoring the spiritual equilibrium of his people. In 1935 he was ordered by the government to refrain from "any activity at public gatherings or closed meetings of Jewish organizations." For three more years he was able to circumvent this order to some extent, as it did not specify his lecturing, until finally in 1938 he was silenced altogether. In March of that year, after five years of fruitful activity under the most trying circumstances, he emigrated with his family to Palestine.

During these years of teaching and lecturing at the University of Frankfurt and in public, Buber developed his philosophy of education, which had always occupied a central place in his social thinking and communal work. He was particularly active in the field of adult education, which he helped to promote in the general German as well as in the Jewish community. However, his views on education as a conscious endeavor in the development of man deal primarily with the formative character of the child and youth. His philosophy of education centers on the problem of freedom, which is paramount in the mind of individual man today. What is the child educated to, what forces in him are being released in the educative process, and what is the role of the educator in this process? Most important, what part does man's drive for freedom play in this entire enterprise, and is freedom as such its real goal? The answer depends on what is meant by freedom. Buber notes two aspects of it.

There is an inner freedom of decision, and there is an outer freedom from interference. The first is freedom *to* act in a positive sense in direction of man's destiny, that is, to realize one's humanity through *communion* with others. The second is freedom *from* outside pressure, that is, in a negative sense, not to act under *compulsion*. Communion and compulsion are thus the two poles of man's freedom of action, and freedom as such oscillates between them positively or negatively. The true human goal is communion without compulsion, and freedom in a positive way means the possibility of entering into relation. In itself, therefore, freedom does nothing and is not a goal, yet without it there can be no real communion. When the bonds of tradition that have been built up through the generations are loosened, man may feel free in an illusory, negative way. He may feel relieved of the old ties and compulsions, but he may also be left without direction, that is, not free to act. "To become free of a bond," Buber says, "is destiny. . . . Let us realize the true meaning of being free of a bond: it means that a quite personal responsibility takes the place of one shared with many generations. Life lived in freedom is personal responsibility or it is a pathetic farce."[53]

[53]*Between Man and Man*, p. 92.

As Buber sees the task of education today, it is a matter of replacing the crumbling bonds of the past with ever greater responsibility on the part of each person by himself, for there may be little else left for him to lean on. It would serve no purpose to try to imbue him with absolute values or norms which have lost their meaning to him. There must be a new start from something latent in man himself, and that is his desire to become a person. This desire is to be awakened "by pointing to the relation of the individual to his own self,"[54] which is the function of the educator. But what is man in himself that lends itself to this educative process? Buber rejects every attempt made by modern psychologists to reduce human character to a single trait, drive, or other primal element, such as "libido" or "will to power."[55] Man has many drives or instincts. However, from the educator's point of view, two of the instincts are to be cultivated with special care, and these are what Buber designates as the "instinct of origination" and the "instinct for communion." The first is a striving to make things originally, to share in the becoming of the world of things around, in general. The second is "the longing for the world to become present to us as a person. . . ."[56]

Man's goal is to become a unified self or realize himself as a whole being and thus to attain also a unified society. Indeed, man cannot realize himself except through his communion with others, and this inborn communality in him is the force that engenders community. If society is to be renewed as a vital com-

[54]*Ibid.,* p. 110.
[55]*Ibid.,* p. 85.
[56]*Ibid.,* pp. 85, 88.

munity, therefore, there must be a restructuring of relations between its members, and this in turn can be achieved only through education as a persuasive force, not through compulsion by the state or any other agency. To be sure the educator is to foster the origina- tor instinct of the child, but that in itself does not make man the unified self or person he yearns to be. "An edu- cation based only on the training of the instinct of origi- nation would prepare a new human solitariness which would be the most painful of all."[57] This instinct teaches us to see the world of things as objects, things to be made, but not as subjects which we may choose and be chosen by, confirm and be confirmed by. The latter perception is attained by the instinct for communion. The two instincts together, when released through the process of education and allowed to exercise their full potentialities freely, will bring about the restructuring of our society as a true community.

The community which Buber hopes will emerge in this restructuring process is one in which the govern- ment does not exercise excessive power over its citizens in order to keep their inner contending forces from dis- rupting the communal structure or to prevent outer hostile forces from subduing it. To use a term which Buber applied to the social structures of Proudhon and Kropotkin, his concept of state is that of an *anocracy*, that is, not the abolition of the state but its nondomi- nance in the social life of the community. For Buber is neither an anarchist nor a utopian. His social vision is that of "religious socialism," as he understood these two terms: *religio*, a person's self-binding to God, which

[57]*Ibid.*, p. 87.

can be realized only through communion with fellowman, and *socialitas*, the formation of human fellowship,
which is possible only through a common relationship
to God.[58] He sees in human society a tension between
what he calls the "political principle" and the "social
principle," and cautions against the accumulation of the
former in the hands of the government, which may turn
it into an oppressive force. It is only when the social
principle predominates that society can function as a
true community, and such a community is at its best
when it is structured out of small communities com-
bined into larger ones in national or territorial units.
The interhuman relations in this structure are neither
individualistic nor collectivist, but represent communality—a relationship of person with person, each confirming the other through mutual response and responsibility.[59]

In the Modern Mode of Thinking

"It is often argued," Buber noted, "whether I am a
philosopher, a theologian or whatever else. . . . As far
as I know myself I would call myself an atypical
man."[60] To this may be added his other favorite self-
appraisal, that he is a "philosophizing man," as differentiated from the philosophizing system-builder. He

[58] *Pointing the Way*: Three Theses of a Religious Social-
ism, pp. 112–114.
[59] *Paths in Utopia*, pp. 132 ff.; *Pointing the Way*: The
Validity and Limitation of the Political Principle, pp. 208 ff.;
The Knowledge of Man: Elements of the Interhuman.
The Social and the Interhuman, pp. 72 ff., Imposition and
Unfolding, pp. 82 f.; *Between Man and Man*: What Is Man?
Prospect, pp. 199–205.
[60] *Werke* I, p. 1111.

does not seek to build a metaphysical "home" in which man may find shelter for all his doubts. Yet he regards as the real problem of the modern human crisis not man's homelessness but rather man's unreadiness to accept his status in an open world in which his destiny has placed him in our time. Buber's philosophy may thus be characterized as "open-ended"—anchored in man's finite being and from there reaching out towards a meeting with infinite Divine Being. Like all humanists, Buber starts with man, but, unlike many others, he does not end with man as an absolute, even though he recognizes him as a being *sui generis*. Buber's absolute is the Eternal Thou, not the human Thou. He calls his outlook "a believing humanism," but it differs from similar outlooks in many ways, in both their humanistic and their believing aspects. Buber himself has dwelt on these differences in his discussions of a number of his contemporaries and predecessors. A brief description of these differences will help to define his place in the modern trends of thought.[61]

The concept of a believing humanism, as such, Buber patterned after ERASMUS, but with the following differentiating remarks. In Erasmus' view, he said, there

---

[61]I am presenting here Buber's discussions of the philosophers as he sees their anthropological views of man in relation to his own anthropology. In this short Introduction I cannot treat the broader implications of their divergencies. See in P. A. Schilpp and M. Friedman, eds., *The Philosophy of Martin Buber*: Nathan Rotenstreich, "The Right and the Limitations of Buber's Dialogical Thought:" Background and Motives, pp. 112 ff.; Fritz Kaufmann, "Martin Buber's Philosophy of Religion:" Buber Among the Philosophers, pp. 205–213; Jean Wahl, "Martin Buber and the Philosophies of Existence," pp. 475 ff. See also Maurice Friedman. *Martin Buber: The Life of Dialogue*, pp. 217–220, 271–274.

are two principles in man's life, one of "natural humanity" in earthly life and the other of "belief" through which man separates himself from this life and rises high above to the Divine. In Buber's own view there is no such separation. On the contrary, man's striving toward the Divine is inconceivable without the natural impulses. Man reaches God not through some special spiritual faculty but with his whole being.

FEUERBACH, says Buber, "introduced that discovery of the *Thou*, which has been called 'the Copernican revolution' of modern thought, and 'an elemental happening which is just as rich in consequences as the idealist discovery of the I'. . . ."[62] In his *Principles of the Philosophy of the Future* Feuerbach proclaims truth to be not in thinking but "in the totality of man's life and essence." Also, "True dialectic is not a monologue of the solitary thinker with himself; it it a dialogue between I and Thou." Furthermore, the essence of man is not in the individual by himself; it "is contained only in the community, in the unity of man with man—a unity, though, which rests only on the reality of the difference between I and Thou."[63] We have here the basic ingredients of Buber's own philosophy of the dialogic principle. However, Feuerbach sees man only in existential relation to fellowman, not to God. At best, he conceives the primal interhuman relationship as divine, which is a humanization of God or, as Buber calls it, "the substitution of an anthropological ersatz God." In Feuerbach's words, "Man for himself is man

---

[62]*Between Man and Man*, p. 148. Buber quotes Karl Heim, *Glaube und Denken*, Erste Auflage, 1931, pp. 305 ff.

[63]Ludwig Feuerbach, *Grundsätze der Philosophie der Zukunft*, # #58, 59, 62.

(in the usual sense); man with man—the unity of I and Thou is God."[64] This, he maintains, is attained through communality, not through solitude. Although both agree on the communal aspect of the relation, Buber regards the I-Thou dialogue as "a free partnership" between man and God, who are mutually independent beings, though the Divine is infinite and entirely transcendent to the human, who is finite. In their meeting there is an intersection of all interhuman relations. The meeting between man and God is the same as that between man and man; the latter is limited by the fact that every Thou may be—nay, must be—turned into an It, whereas in the former the Thou can never become an It.[65]

Another modern thinker who left his deeply religious mark on Buber from his youth was SÖREN KIERKE-GAARD, who saw the relationship between man and God as that of "the single one" to the absolute. That is, the essence of man's existence is that he himself alone (*der Einzelne*) is summoned by God to enter into relation with Him. Kierkegaard considers man's relation with man, that is, his communal aspect, as well as his relation with the world, a hindrance to his relation with God. Thus, says Buber, he conceived of "the highest essential relationship" but not on the human level. In Buber's view, the latter is of man's essence, for he cannot reach God except through his communality with fellowman.[66]

---

[64]*Ibid.*, #60. *Cf. Between Man and Man*, p. 210.
[65]*Cf. Between Man and Man*, pp. 213–214, on the clarification of this concept in Buber's own thinking.
[66]*Ibid.*, "The Question to the Single One," pp. 41 ff. See also p. 211.

NIETZSCHE, as stated above, exerted great influence on Buber, but only during his early formative years. When Buber succeeded in shaking off the "rousing influence" of "Zarathustra," he took issue with his predecessor's announcement of the "death of God" and the social implications of "the will to power." Buber recognizes Nietzsche's contribtuion toward resolving the anthropological question "What is man?" by placing it in reference to time and the eternal. But, says Buber, Nietzsche conceives of the human species as part of the rest of nature whirling in an eternally recurrent cycle of time, which does not at all assure the perfection that the philosopher holds out for supreme man. For it is only by chance that some members of this species may reach that stage, but upon reaching it will find that an ever-surpassing will to power is a false image of superiority. From a psychological and historical viewpoint, power can be conceived properly only as a means to an end; those who seek it as an end in itself show weakness rather than strength. Nietzsche's attempt to make "the will to power" the new measure of all values and thus to rescue modern man from nihilism was only a futile effort to replace God, whom he declared dead, by other gods who must issue from within man himself.[67]

In the same vein Buber takes issue with SARTRE, who seeks meaning in human existence after having done away with God's existence. "That," Buber notes, "is almost exactly what Nietzsche said, and it has not become any truer since then."[68] The issue centers main-

[67]*Eclipse of God*, p. 111; *Between Man and Man*, pp. 148 ff.
[68]*Eclipse of God*, p. 70.

ly on the role of freedom in man's destiny. Sartre holds that the very existence of God deprives man of his freedom, for he cannot say "no" to a Supreme Being whose decisions cannot be questioned. In Buber's view, however, "man is not a blind tool; he is created as a free being, free also in encounter with God, free to submit or deny himself to Him. Man gives an independent answer to God's sovereign address; even when he is silent, it is an answer."[69]

In a conversation with MAX SCHELER a few years after World War I, that is, after Buber had already undergone a transformation in his religious life, Scheler said to him: "I have come very near your narrow ridge." By this he meant the mystic view which Buber, following Meister Eckhart and the Kabbala, had held in his early period, namely, that "the primal ground (*Urgrund*) of being, the nameless, impersonal godhead, comes to 'birth' in the human soul," or in the "realization of God through man." Buber pointed out that he had given up this idea a long time ago, whereas Scheler had just embraced it and "surpassed it by his idea of a 'becoming of God.' "[70]

Both philosophers try to meet the demand of our time for a philosophical anthropology. "In no other age," Scheler states, "have the views about the being and origin of man been more uncertain, indefinite and varied than in ours . . . we are the first age in which man has become fully and thoroughly a 'problematic' unto himself, in that he no longer knows what he is, but at the same time knows that he doesn't know it."[71]

---

[69]*Der Jude und sein Judentum*, p. 173.
[70]*Between Man and Man*, pp. 184–185.
[71]*Cf.* Max Scheler, *Philosophische Weltanschauung* (Bonn, 1929), p. 15.

Buber appreciates the manner in which Scheler poses the philosophical problem of man but says that his anthropology is not of the whole human being but is only a certain manifestation of it. Scheler derives his anthropology from the essence of man's being as such, which he then applies to the absolute ground of all being or the world-ground. He endows this ground with two attributes, one an endless *spirit* and the other an irrational *drive*. Insofar as the first becomes involved in the second and spiritualizes it, God comes into being. When Scheler looks again at man, whose anthropology he had just dissected, he finds that man is none other than the spiritual attribute of the absolute or world-ground manifest in the human person, from which this attribute was derived to begin with. The absolute being is not in itself an actuality, not an existing god, but a godhood or *deitas* in eternal becoming in historical time. It realizes itself in the history of man, which is the only place where godhood becomes manifest.[72]

The main burden of Scheler's doctrine is that, of the two prime attributes of the world-ground, the drive is active and creative and the spirit is passive and powerless. First of all, says Buber, this powerless spirit is not an ontic reality manifest in man, as Scheler contends. Second, if it spiritualizes the forces of the drive, it can only have the effect of debilitating the latter. Third, inasmuch as the essence of man, according to this anthropology, is his spiritual quality, he emerges from it as a passive being, " 'a potential direction of a process,' " not a real living man.[73]

---

[72]*Cf.* Max Scheler, "Die Sonderstellung des Menschen," *Mensch und Erde*, Herausgegeben von Hermann Keyserling (Darmstadt, 1927), pp. 225–226.

[73]*Between Man and Man*, pp. 183–195.

HEIDEGGER's man as a present being (*Dasein*) related to its own being, says Buber, is not real man but "a metaphysical homunculus."[74] If Kierkegaard places the existence of man in the "single one" who enters into relation with God, Heidegger finds this existence in "solitary man," as related not to a Divine Other or any "other" but rather to his own self. This "radically solitary man," says Buber, represents not the whole human life but only a certain condition of the human predicament in our time. Heidegger absolutizes it "and wants to derive the essence of human existence from the experience of a nightmare."[75] The essence of his man is the individual as such, who becomes a "resolved" self in himself. His "self is *a closed system*."[76] This man is alone, standing before himself and nothing else. Since in living reality this is impossible, man stands in his dread before nothing.

Buber does not discuss the RADICAL THEOLOGIANS of the God-is-dead persuasion directly, but his reply to their speculations is that they cannot accept God as the Wholly Other who is transcendent to man, and that they look to an apocalyptic end of the world of creation and to the emergence of a new, most perfect world. God the creator of the world of nature, they contend, cannot by his very Being as creator bring about this new spiritualized world. He must, therefore, die or be killed, in order to allow the latter to emerge out of His nothingness.[77]

[74]*Ibid.*, p. 182.
[75]*Ibid.*, p. 168.
[76]*Ibid.*, p. 171. See further, pp. 172–175, for a detailed comparison between Kierkegaard's "single one" and Heidegger's "solitary man."
[77]*Der Jude und sein Judentum*, p. 173. *Cf. Israel and the World*, p. 36, on the apocalyptic end of days.

Although BERGSON exerted an influence on Buber's
development, the concept of intuition, which is usually
associated with the philosophies of both, is not the same
in the two cases. Nor is the former's view that intellectual knowledge falsifies reality shared by the latter. Essentially, Bergson regards intuition as an act of overcoming the duality of observer and observed, that is, of
bridging the gap between the knowing subject and the
object known. Buber, on the other hand, accepts this
duality as an ontic state which is not abolished or even
diminished in the intuitive act. On the contrary, the
dual presence of observer and observed is the basis of
the primal communion between them, which may be
characterized as intuition. In Buber's language this is
the same as the direct, immediate experience of relation. In his view, intuition is not a special capacity but
a state of relation "where our whole being becomes one
in the act of knowing," but not the oneness of knower
and known. For Bergson, intuition is a plunging into
the experienced event where we act but do not see ourselves acting, that is, we do not see ourselves as separate from the object of our cognitive act, or the act of
knowing and the object known are as one in the stream
of pure duration. It is this concept of time in human
experience that constitutes the demarcation line between the two philosophers. For Bergson, time as duration is a flowing present, and the intuitive act merges
the observer and the observed into this flowing stream.
For Buber, time in man's experience is always of the
past, as given in memory. As soon as memory sets in,
however, the unity is broken.[78] Although Buber denies
the claim which Bergson makes for intuition, he says

[78]*Between Man and Man*, p. 141.

that "it remains his great service that he, as no other thinker of our day, has directed our attention to intuition."[79]

Buber's reaction to MARX's view of man is related to the anthropological question "What is man?" and to the problem of the restructuring of society.[80] Marx sees real man as the producer of material conditions of life, and his social relations as a manifestation of the relationships of production. In his words, "the mode of production of the material means of existence conditions the whole process of social, political, and intellectual life." As these material forces of production develop, they engender inner antagonisms, which have been overcome at each stage in a progressive line of advancement from time immemorial to our own day. However, at each stage new antagonisms arose on a more intensive level as the productive relationships progressed. The goal that Marx sees for man is the abolition of all antagonisms, or the establishment of the kind of relations of production which will no longer engender social conflicts. This, he says, will be accomplished by the proletariat as it abolishes the present bourgeois order of productive relationships, for this order, according to Marx, is the last stage of the antagonistic forms of the social forces of production.[81]

[79] *Pointing the Way*: "Bergson's Concept of Intuition," p. 86.
[80] *Between Man and Man*, pp. 143–145. *Paths in Utopia*: "Marx and the Renewal of Society." pp. 80–98.
[81] Karl Marx, "A Contribution to 'The Critique of Political Economy,' " Author's Preface, in Emile Burns, ed., *A Handbook of Marxism* (New York: International Publishers, 1935), pp. 371–373. Note Lenin's elaboration, pp. 544 ff.

What is noteworthy in this advent of the Marxian perfect society is that it is to come about as a natural process through the dialectic of the forces of production as such. That is, these forces will of necessity lead to the inner breakdown of the bourgeois order, out of which the new perfect society will emerge with predictable inevitability. It is this "certainty with regard to perfection" as a natural process that prompted Buber to reject Marx's view of man's destiny in general. He grants that the renewal of society will come through the forces of social life, as it does in all life, but not "with the necessity of a natural process," as Marx predicts.[82] Rather, the future depends on man's decision regarding the direction that these forces will take. Development in itself, as conceived in terms of cosmological, that is, impersonal, time, does not lead to a perfect human order, for it may also go in the opposite direction, toward decay and destruction. Marx disregards the factor of human decision as an originating power, and wants to guarantee absolute security in the new social structure as coming from the natural forces of the proletariat.

Buber sees man's position in the world of nature as insecure when it comes to future prediction. "The anthropological concept of man . . . ," he states, "cannot be understood simply as a part of the [natural] world. Within the boundaries of the human world which is given in the problem of human being there is no certainty of the future." Dialectics of the natural process is therefore no guarantee against failure. Man himself, perhaps in his deepest state of insecurity, can lift him-

[82]*Between Man and Man*, p. 144.

self out of it by answering "with his decision the question about man's being." As to the perfection of society in the future, no human being can guarantee it. When man decides to go in this direction, he will also have faith or trust in the Eternal Guarantor for all that "has not yet come to be in our world."[83]

Buber and His Readers

In 1951 Buber retired from active teaching at the Hebrew University. Seven years later his wife died, and he went to live with his granddaughter, Mrs. Barbara Goldschmidt, in Jerusalem. He continued his creative work in the fields of his life-long interests. It was not until 1961, at the age of eighty-three and after thirty-six years of concentrated work, that he finished his German translation of the Bible; and only a few months before he died, on June 13, 1965, he selected the series of essays which went into his last book, *Nachlese*, published posthumously the same year.[84]

Buber's influence was great and widespread among philosophers, theologians, and men of practical affairs during his lifetime and has continued to grow among ever wider circles since his death. But his impact on people was greatest through his spoken word, his personal relationships and through his very extensive correspondence. Richard Scheimann, who translated his *Kingship of God*, relates having "once met Martin Buber" at a private gathering in Chicago. "I do not remember anything that was said on that occasion," Schei-

[83]*Ibid.*, pp. 141, 145.
[84]See its English translation by Maurice Friedman, *A Believing Humanism: My Testament 1902–1965*.

mann wrote in the Introduction to his translation. "I came away that evening convinced that I had met a genuine charismatic." Professor Shmuel Hugo Bergmann, one of Buber's closest friends, described him in the following words: "For he was a man of love in a hate-ridden world, a man of large vision in a short-sighted age. At a time when human relations had become anonymous and matter-of-fact he taught us that salvation can only be found in the renewal of relations between the I and Thou in the life of individuals as well as in the life of nations."[85]

A most fitting characterization of the life and work of the man who spoke the word-pair I-Thou to fellow-man we find in a statement addressed to his readers. In his Foreword to his book *Pointing the Way* Buber asks the reader to bear in mind the stages "I had to pass through before I could enter into an independent relationship with being." And having reached the stage of relation, he says to those who will confront him in his writings: "Being true to the being in which and before which I am placed is the one thing that is needful. . . . The readers for whom I hope are those who see my way as one, parallel to their own way towards true existence."

[85]Shmuel H. Bergmann, "Buber: A Sentinel of Mankind," *The Jewish News*, Newark, N.J., July 1, 1966, p. 12.

Analytical Interpretation

PART ONE:

Man's Twofold Communication with the World

1. *The Two Primary Words* [53–54]*

"To man the world is twofold, according to his twofold communication."† Man communicates with the world in two ways. He may address that which is not himself, the other, as *Thou* or as *It*, that is, he may speak I-Thou or I-It. The "other" is the same in both instances, but the communication established is not the same. Nor is the one who says I-It fully the same as the one who says I-Thou. These two ways of speaking are designated as "primary words" (*Grundworte*). They are actually not single words but word-pairs, I-Thou

---

*The numbers in brackets after each section heading and subheading refer to pages in *I and Thou*, Martin Buber. A new translation, with prologue and notes, by Walter Kaufmann. New York: Charles Scribner's Sons, 1970. For corresponding page numbers in the Second Edition of Ronald Gregor Smith's translation (New York, 1958), see p. 149 in this book.

†His twofold communication. The German reads *nach seiner zwiefältigen Haltung.* I translated *Haltung* as "communication" rather than "attitude." Buber seeks to establish the ontological basis of man's communication with fellowman, nature, and God, not his psychological reaction to reality, which the word "attitude" connotes. The German word *Haltung* is to be taken here in the sense of *sich zu einem halten*, "to be associated or in communion with someone, to keep one's company." Buber uses *Kommunion* and *kommunizieren* in the same sense as the English "communication" (*cf. Werke* I, 392–393).

and I-It. The word He or She may take the place of
It. Each word-pair represents a specific relationship
of man to the world, and the relationship of one pair
is not like that of the other. Accordingly, when one
speaks I he means either I-It or I-Thou, for whenever
I is spoken it implies the second word of one or the
other pair.

The primary words do not predicate anything about
what may exist outside of them, but when spoken they
establish a state of relationship, that is, an existent. They
are spoken out of man's very being. Yet only the I-Thou
may be spoken with one's full being; the I-It can never
be spoken so fully. If one wants to know who is the
I, he must not take it as a single word by itself, but
within one of the two word-pairs. The I is either of the
I-Thou or of the I-It, and since the two word-pairs do
not stand for the same relationship, the I of one is also
different from that of the other. "To be I and to speak
I are one. To speak I and to speak one of the primary
words are one. He who speaks the primary word, takes
his stand in the word." (8).‡

2. *Experience and Relation: Three Spheres* [54–56]

"The life of a human being is not circumscribed by
transitive verbs alone. It does not consist only of acts
which have a thing for their object" (8). The world
of It is constituted of objects delimiting each other.

‡The numbers in parentheses in the text are page references to quotations from *Ich und Du* in the volume *Das
dialogische Prinzip*, Martin Buber. Heidelberg: Verlag Lambert Schneider, 1962.

Whenever man has an object before him, be it an object of percepetion, imagination, will, or thought, he has established the realm of It, the realm of his experience (*Erfahrung*). But the world of Thou is different. "One who speaks Thou does not have some thing as his object. . . . Thou does not delimit. . . . It has nothing. But it stands in the relation (*Beziehung*)" (8).

"It is said, man experiences his world." Whether the experience is inner or outer, secret or open, the thing experienced is known to him through its component elements, through some parts that belong to it. But the experience, as such, is not in the thing but in man. It arises in him and not between him and the world. In this experience neither side partakes of the other. The world does nothing in the process of experience; it neither helps nor hinders, nor does it suffer anything from it. "The world of experience belongs to the primary word I-It. The primary word I-Thou establishes the world of relation." (9).

The world of relation, that is, of I-Thou, arises in three spheres. (1) *In life with nature*, where the relation is below the level of speech. Creatures may reach out to us but cannot come over to us. Our saying Thou to them remains on the threshold of speech. (2) *In life with people*, where the relation may be found through speech; we can say and hear Thou. (3) *In life with spiritual beings*, where the relation is beyond the use of speech, but where speech is intimated in its revelation; we do not hear Thou but become aware of being addressed, and we respond by forming, thinking, acting. We speak the primary word with our being though not with our lips.

"But how do we venture to bring what is outside

speech into the primary word of relation (10)?" In
each of the three spheres we meet the fringe of the
eternal Thou. We are aware of him in every sphere,
and whenever we say Thou we address ourselves to the
eternal one. (This will be developed in Part Three.)

3. *The Four Potencies of Man's Communication: Cognition, Love, Art, and Faith*

A. TWO WAYS OF CONSIDERING A TREE: COGNITION [56–59]

1. As an Object of Experience. I can regard a
tree as a picture, a movement of foliage, a species, or
a sample of a structure of interacting forces or of component elements. I can conceive it as a number and
abstract it in pure mathematical relationships. In all
these instances the tree remains my object, an It, and
as such has its place and time, its condition and quality.

2. As a Thou in Relation with an I. After I have
considered the tree as an It or object, it may happen
that I have been overcome by the power of its exclusiveness and become involved with it in the sphere of
relation, in I-Thou and no longer in I-It. This does not
eliminate any of the qualities and conditions in the tree
as an object. That is, I need not disregard or forget
what I learned about it through my observation. On the
contrary, all its elements and qualities, mechanical,
chemical, and otherwise, in all their comprehensiveness,
come into the sphere of relation between me and the
tree as a whole. But they are in the relation as a whole,
not in their parts. The tree is not a figment of my imagi-

nation, but is embodied opposite me and is concerned with me as I am with it. Relation is mutuality, I-Thou in reciprocal direction, and this is not to be minimized even though I do not know whether the tree has a consciousness similar to mine. I do not meet in the tree a soul or a dryad, but the tree itself.

B. TWO WAYS OF CONSIDERING FELLOWMAN: LOVE [59–60]

As in the case of the tree, I may stand opposite a man not as my object of observation, but as one whom I address as Thou. He is not then a He or a She delimited by another he or she, like a point in space and time, nor is he a bundle of qualities to be described and experienced. He stands opposite me in his fulness as a Thou, not, to be sure, as if nothing else were there, but as if everything else lived with him. This relation is love, that is, I stand in relation to him as a whole. If I single out any aspect of him for observation or classification, or for some use, he is no longer Thou.

The man to whom I say Thou is not met in some specific time or place, just as prayer is not in time, but time is in prayer, and sacrifice is not in place, but place is in sacrifice, that is, time and place are determined by prayer and sacrifice and not the other way around. When I do (as indeed I must) set the man in time and place, he is not my Thou any more, but a He, a She, or an It. As long as the Thou confronts me, there is no causality or fate to determine me, for I am not determined by the Thou. I do not experience the man to whom I say Thou, but stand in the relation, that is, in the primary word I-Thou. When I step out of it, I experience him. Relation may prevail even when the man whom I address as Thou is not aware of it, for he himself may be in a state of experiencing. The Thou is and does more and receives more than the It may know, for the Thou is fulness of being, whereas the It is not. "Herein deception does not hold; here is the cradle of Real Life" (13).

C. FORM AND FORMATION: ART [60–62]

The eternal prime source of art is a form that confronts man and desires to become a work through him. The form does not arise out of his soul but is an appearance that approaches it and demands its efficient power. Then it becomes a matter of an act of man's being. If man fulfils the act and speaks the primary word to the form with his whole being, the efficient power streams forth and the form becomes a work. The act entails a sacrifice and a risk. In forming an exclusive work, the act of being must sacrifice all other possibilities that run through the perspective of the appearing form. None of those other possibilities may enter the work. This is demanded by the exclusiveness of the confrontation. The art form, like any other Thou, is an exclusive being. The risk is that, inasmuch as the primary word can be spoken only with the whole being, I must give myself to it without withholding of myself in the slightest. Unlike the tree or man whom I may meet, the work of art does not tolerate me to sidetrack into the world of I-It. When confronting man, it comes only in one way, as Thou. It demands my fulfilment of the act of being, my entering-in-relation with it; otherwise it is broken or it breaks me.

"I cannot experience or describe the confronting form; I can only render it actual" (14). And yet, I behold it more clearly than anything in the world of experience, not, however, as a thing among other things, or as a reflection of the imagination, but as that which is present. As a form it cannot be experienced as an It and therefore cannot be described, measured, or calculated; it can only be realized in actuality and become a work of art. The form is present even though it is not "there" as an object, for it is there, present in relation. I stand in real relation to it; it affects me and I affect it by my act of forming the work of art. But when the work of art has been made, it is a thing among things, a sum of properties that may be experienced and described. "Making is creating, inventing is finding, forming is revealing. In rendering actual I discover; I bring the form over into the world of It" (14).

In sum, one experiences nothing of the Thou, for the Thou is not to be experienced. Yet one knows everything about it, for knowledge of the Thou is not a knowledge of single components; one knows it as a whole in the very act of entering-in-relation with it.

The fourth potency, faith, will be discussed in Sections 11, 12b, and 35.

4. *Mediation and Immediacy*

A. MEETING AS AN ACT OF BEING [62–63]

"All real living is meeting." I cannot find the Thou by searching for it; it meets me by grace (*von Gnaden*). It is a relation of choosing and being chosen, action and passion in one. When action is with the being as a whole, which is a suspension of all partial and limited actions and their sensations, it becomes like passion, and this is how the primary element I-Thou can be spoken—only with one's being as a whole, when action becomes passion. I cannot fuse all parts into the whole, but neither can it take place without me. I do not mediate between the parts; I become a whole as I enter-in-relation with Thou. "Becoming I, I speak Thou" (15).

"The relation to Thou is immediate" (15). Between I and Thou there stands no concept, foreknowledge, or fantasy, no purpose, desire, or anticipation. Memory and desires themselves are transformed when they enter from isolation into the whole. "All mediation is hindrance. Only when mediation is removed can meeting take place" (16). In relation of I-Thou, mediation has no place or relevance, whether or not *my* Thou becomes an It for some other I. My entering-in-relation is not affected by someone else who may look at me as a thing, an object. The actual demarcation line between mediate and immediate does not lie between experience (*Erfahrung*) and not-experience (*Nichterfahrung*), between the given and the not-given, that is, whether there is a datum of experience or not, or between being and value of what I experience. In each of these regions the demarcation line lies between Thou and It, between a present (*Gegenwart*) and a thing (*Gegenstand*). That is, the difference in each region is between my entering-in-relation and my experiencing, between my two ways of communicating with reality.

B. PAST AND PRESENT [63–65]

The present, in the sense of relation, is not a point marking off time from the future. What is meant here is the actual, full present that arises only as the Thou becomes present, *is there* opposite me, and that takes place *in* the meeting, in the relation of I-Thou. The I of I-It, on the other hand, has no present, only a past. One who experiences and uses things lives in the past, for in experiencing things one has only objects of what has been. An object is something cut off, arrested, stiffened, contained without duration. The present is abiding, enduring. "True beings are lived in the present; objects are of the past" (17).

This fundamental twofold condition cannot be overcome by erecting a superstructure of a world of ideas. We are not dealing here with an I-in-itself or an Existent-in-itself, but with real man, you and I, our life and our world. To real man, the demarcation line between Thou and It cuts through the world of ideas as well. He who is satisfied with experiencing and using things thinks he can escape the surge of nothingness and find comfort in an auxiliary structure or superstructure of ideas. Finding himself always in a state of I-It, that is, of using things and not relating to others as to a Thou, he is removed from the fulness of reality and develops a sense of nothingness. He then tries to form a concept or idea of the real other, which is only a sublimated It, for the concept or idea is also regarded as something to be used and experienced. Such is the mankind of It, just an idea or concept of humanity which one imagines, postulates, or promulgates, but which has nothing in common with living mankind to whom one can truly say Thou. Ideas are no more enthroned above our heads than they are enshrined in them. They float, move about, bump into us. "One who leaves the primary word unspoken is lamentable; but one who, instead, addresses it with a concept or slogan, as if it were its name, is wretched" (18).

C. THE I AFFECTS THE THOU [65–67]

In the three examples examined above—relation with nature, with man, and with art—the last mentioned indicates most obviously that in the immediate relation the I affects the Thou.

(a) In art, the act of being determines the manner in which the form becomes a work. The form fulfils itself through the meeting, entering the world of things, where it continues to act, endlessly becoming It, and again becoming Thou. It becomes embodied out of the flow of spaceless and timeless present into the realm of existence. (b) When I speak Thou to man, the meaning of my effect on the Thou is not so obvious. It is usually misunderstood as an act of feeling, because the relation is one of love. "Feelings accompany the metaphysical and metapsychical fact of love, but they do not constitute it" (18). Love is one and the same, though its accompanying feelings may differ in kind with the person to whom they are attached. Feelings are "owned," but love "happens." "Feelings dwell in man, but man dwells in his love," which is between man and man, and that is so in reality. Love is not something attached to the I so that the Thou becomes its object or content. "It is between the I and Thou." One who does not know this with his being does not know love, even though he calls certain feelings which he experiences and enjoys by that name. "Love is an effect that permeates the world." To the one who stands in it, every man—good or evil, wise or foolish, beautiful or ugly—really becomes a Thou, that is, singularly confronts him as a Thou. In love there arises an exclusiveness which makes one effective, helping, healing, bringing up, lifting up, saving. "Love is responsibility of an I for a Thou." In this, all who love are alike, from the smallest to the greatest. But this is impossible in the case of feeling. (18–19).

D. MUTUAL EFFECT IN RELATION [67–68]

"Relation is mutuality. My Thou affects me as I affect it." But is it correct to say that love is the only potency of entering-in-relation with fellow man, or is it even a good example of human relation, when there is hate in the world? Buber's answer is, "Yes, it is the only potency of real relation." Love may be blind, that is, it may not see the other being. But in that case it does not truly stand in the primary word of relation, in I-Thou, for it cannot "see" the other. On the other hand, hate is never blind in the same sense, for it never sees the whole being to begin with. One who hates, hates only part of a being, but one who sees a whole being and yet rejects it is not in the realm of hate, but rather in human restrictiveness, unable to say Thou, unable to enter-in-relation with the other as a whole. This limitation signifies the relativity of the act of entering-in-relation, and when it is recognized as such it can be removed. "Yet, the one who hates without mediation is nearer to relation than the one who is without love or hate" (20).

E. PASSING FROM THOU TO IT [68–69]

"This, however, is the sublime melancholy of our lot, that every Thou in our world must become an It" (20). The Thou, which has an exclusive present in the immediacy of relation, turns into an object among objects as soon as the relation has been attained or has become mediated. This takes place in all three types of relation. In the work of art, fulfilment in actuality (*Ver-*

wirklichung), in one sense, means the loss of actuality (*Entwirklichung*) in another, that is, when the work is consummated and becomes an It. Similarly, the creature which has just now opened itself up to me in the mystery of mutual activity can now again be described, analyzed, classified according to a manifold of laws, that is, as an object of observation. And in the case of man's communication with man, love itself cannot tarry in the immediacy of relation; its duration fluctuates between the actual and the potential. The man who erstwhile was singular, present, and only to be met as a Thou has now again become a He or a She, a sum of properties, a quantity taking shape in space and time. So long as I can extract from him the color of his hair, his speech, or his goodness, he is no more my Thou.

"It is the destiny of every Thou in the world essentially to become a thing or to be always ready to enter the state of things. In the language of things one would say: Every *thing* in the world, either before or after becoming a thing, is able to appear to an I as its Thou. But the language of things touches only the tip of real life" (21).

5. *Primacy of I-Thou Relation*

A. IN THE LIFE OF PRIMITIVE MAN

1. Living Interaction in Relation [69–73]

"In the beginning was relation" (22). In the life of primitive man relation is expressed in the very mode of his speaking. It is not like our civilized language which indicates analysis and reflection, that is, mediated thought. We respond to one who meets us by greeting him in the name of God or by wishing him well; these are mediated, indirect, worn-out formulas, as compared with the primitive, eternally young, bodied greeting of relation "I see you" or with the American Indian variant, "Smell me!" In primitive life the relation is of body meeting body. The two are in sufficient relief to be distinguishable beings, but they are not separated from each other, one is not outside the other. For relation is not separation, as the true meaning of immediacy signifies.

The same holds true of primitive man's relation to nature. He does not pay attention to the moon, which he sees every night, until it comes down to him in sleep or while he is awake and casts a spell over him for good or for evil. What he retains then is not an optic vision of a disk of light wandering through the sky or of some domestic belonging to it, but a stirring image of lunar action that moves and permeates his body. Then the memory of what was perceived, but was unknown, every night in the sky assumes the image of the agent and carrier of the effect, and makes it possible for Thou to become a He or a She of one's experience. The original relation of primitive man to the moon was body to body. His memory of it may then become a thing of experience. But what now appears to him as a thing had its ground in the I-Thou relation.

Present-day research has noted the origin of the relational character of the appearance of being, although its spiritual element in primitive life has not yet been understood. Some regard this mysterious power as a mode of natural belief or a science of nature-peoples. The belief is here synonymous with a primitive science. It is the power which is expressed in Mana, in Orenda, or even in higher development: in the original meaning of Brahman, the Dynamis, Charis, and magic Papyri, and in the Apostolic Letters. It is regarded as super-sensible or supernatural. But these categories, as we understand them, are not those of the primitives. The latter live within the bounds of bodied interaction, to which visitations from the dead belong quite naturally. The primitive would consider it nonsensical to assume that anything nonsensible exists. The appearances to which he ascribes mystic potency are all elemental events of relation, that is, they are events of which he may form an idea because they stimulate his body and leave a stimulus-image in him.

The sun, the moon, the beasts, the dead, the chief-tain, to which he relates when awake or asleep, have the power of leaving their images in him. That is, this power permeates everything in the world of primitive man, and that is why he considers it magical. It is the magic of nature and not of a special human power which may be different from nature. Furthermore, this magic power is not a causal force acting continuously, but rather a power which bursts forth ever anew, like a volcanic movement, without prediction. Each living relation is a new "living experience" (*Erlebnis*)*, un-predictable and nonrepetitive.

2. Separation of I from Thou [73–75]

Self-trained memory, which turns the Thou into an It, arranges the events of relation in a certain order.

---

*The phrase "living experience" means the relational ex-perience as distinguished from the experience of using. In German the two are differentiated by the words *Erlebnis* (living experience) and *Erfahrung* (experience of using).

This is the formation of an ordered world. (See Section 7 on a world-order and an ordered world.) First, the effects that are most important to the drive for self-preservation and most significant to the drive for cognition come to the fore most strongly, are separated, and are objectified. Second, the less important, that is, the changing Thou of the living interaction, which comes and goes, and comes again in a different guise, but never the same, steps back, remains isolated in memory, and objectifies itself gradually into groups and species, each group of objects being the memory of a Thou. Third, the unchanging partner, the I, comes forth, awesome in its separation, like a ghost but undeniably distinct. This I is separated from the original I-Thou relation but not yet formed into an I-It experience. I become aware of the I, but not through my drives. The consciousness of the I is not dominant in the drive of self-preservation or in any other drive. It is not the I that wants to propagate itself but the body, which is yet unaware of an I. Not the I but the body wants to make things, tools, toys, wants to become a progenitor (*Urheber*). Similarly, in the primitive cognitive function one cannot find a *cognosco ergo sum* ("I think; therefore I am"), even in its most naive form or in the most childish conception of an experiencing subject. "The 'I' arises in elemental form out of the separation of the primary living interactions, out of the primary words *I-affecting-Thou* and *Thou-affecting-I*, after the participle has been objectified, hypostatized into a substance" (25). When the affecting becomes an object, the I turns into its subject: I am affecting something. The affecting becomes something affected. But this I has been singled out of the original I-Thou relation. It has no independent existence, as such; it can exist only as a subject to an object in I-It. Nor does it have a pre-existence by itself; it existed in the I-Thou, and now it exists in I-It. There is no other I except in the two primary word-pairs. But of the two, the I-Thou has the primacy; the I-It is formed out of it.

3. Formation of I-It [75–76]

This is the fundamental difference in the way the primary words are spoken by primitive man. He says I-Thou before forming an image of himself as an I. When the I is separated from the Thou, as described above, he speaks I-It, thus recognizing himself as I in connection with an object. I-Thou is thus decomposed into I and Thou, but in itself it did not arise as a composite of the two; the original act is I-Thou. On the other hand, I-It arose out of a combination or composition of I, when separated from I-Thou, and It, when the Thou became objectified as an object of the I. The I-Thou is anterior to the becoming of I (*Vorichhaft*); the I-It is posterior to the becoming of I (*Nachichhaft*) (26).

There are two partners in the primitive relational event, man and his encounter. As the world becomes in this event a dual system, man becomes the I, although he has no inner awareness of it as a separate existent. "In the primitive relational event, the I is included by its very exclusiveness" (26). Now the actual event which passes into the primary word I-It, as an experience with reference to an I, does not yet include the I as an experiencing subject. The actual event is the separation of the human body from its environment, the body as the bearer of its perceptions and the surrounding world as juxtaposed to it. But this differentiation of pure juxtaposition does not imply an I, as such. In the I-Thou relation, the I is included as an exclusive being which encounters an "other" exclusive being, the Thou. Man senses the I but is not conscious of it as a separate existent, for he is in the relational event as a whole. When the I-Thou passes over into the experience of I-It, the I is not included in this experience forthwith. There is a transitional stage in which the human body differentiates itself from the outside world as the bearer of sensations through which the world is experienced. It is the body, then, which is first identified as I-subject juxtaposed to the world as It-object. Then this sensing I appears as a separate existing I-subject.

As the I of relation in the I-Thou emerges and becomes a separate existent, it also penetrates as an attenuated, functional factor into the actual event of the body's separation from its environment. Only then can there arise the conscious act of I, the first form of the primary word I-It, which is directed toward subjective experience. Only then does the I become aware of itself as an experiencing subject. The emergent I declares itself as the bearer of the perceptions attributed to the body. This takes place in primitive form, not as a theory of knowledge. But when the sentence "I see the tree" is so stated that it no longer indicates a relation between a man-I and a tree-Thou, but designates rather an experience of a tree-object by a man-consciousness, that statement has erected a barrier between a subject and an object. "The primary word I-It, the word of separation, has been spoken" (27).

It seems, then, as if "that melancholy of our lot originated in primitive history." This is so insofar as the conscious life of man itself originated in primeval history. But the conscious life only reflects the world of being in human becoming. The spirit appears in time as a product, even as a by-product, of nature, and yet it is this spirit which envelops nature timelessly. "The contrast between the two primary words has had many names in different times and worlds; but in its nameless truth it is inherent in creation" (27). In that case, one may ask, is one to believe in a paradise of mankind's hoary past? Not necessarily. Even if the past was hell—and it certainly was full of terror and cruelty—it was not unreal. "But far better is violence in real living experiences of being than the phantom solicitudes of faceless numbers! From the one a way leads to God; from the other only into nothingness" (28).

B. IN THE LIFE OF THE CHILD

1. Striving for Relation is A Priori [76–78]

The life of primitive man, even if we were able to unlock it more fully, represents actual primitive man only by analogy. From primitive life, therefore, we gain only a glimpse of the temporal connection of the two primary words. More complete information we receive from the life of the child. Here it is unveiled most clearly that the spiritual reality of the primary words arises from the naturally disposed union of the I-Thou, on one hand, and from the naturally disposed separation of I-It, on the other.

The prenatal life of the child is a union of pure natural disposition, a reciprocal action flowing from one body to another, the one drawn into the other and yet not entirely in it, for the child does not lie in the lap of the human mother only. The union is world-embracing, as if the child read the entire primordial script, suggesting the Jewish legend that in the mother's womb man knows everything and at the moment of birth forgets it all. Man retains this image of world-knowledge as a hidden yearning to return, not, to be sure, to the mother's womb, but to the world-embracing union of his now emerged spiritual being with true Thou.

"Every human child that comes into being, like all beings in the process of becoming, rests in the lap of the great mother—the undivided, unshaped primordial world from which it cuts itself loose unto personal life" (29). But the severing does not occur suddenly and catastrophically like the one from the physical mother. Man is granted a given period for the establishment of spiritual connection with the world, that is, relation, in place of the natural one. Relation is thus the spiritual tie which comes into existence when I-Thou is spoken. According to Buber, spirit is not a substance or a being, but a relation, a between, which comes into being in the human act of entering-in-relation, in meeting. (This will be developed more fully in Section 8b.) "Creation reveals its formative modes through meeting. It does not pour itself into the expectant senses; it encounters the one who seizes upon" (29).

The origin of striving for relation shows itself on the earliest, most inchoate level. Before even the child perceives an individual thing, it may look into empty space, toward something undefined, stretch its hand as if grasping something indeterminate. After many trials the glance may rest on a red carpet design and not be moved until the soul of redness reveals itself; or the hand may touch the teddy-bear and the child may thus become innerly aware of a body, a determinate form. In both instances the experience is not of an object, but of something that is met, to be sure only in fantasy, and that exerts a living effect. This fantasy, however, is not at all a general animation of things. "It is the drive to make everything a Thou, the drive toward general relation" (30). When the opposite, that which is encountered, is not a living being but only an image or symbol, the living effect is completed out of the child's own being. Gradually the child will also start to speak with the opposite, be it only to prattle with a simmering teakettle.

The child does not first perceive a "thing" and then set himself in relation to it. On the contrary, the striving for relation is primal: the cupped hand in which the "other" snuggles up is first; the setting in relation with it, which is a silent protoform of saying Thou, is second. A still later occurrence is the emerging of a thing out of the decomposition of the primary living interaction, out of the separation of the united partners, the same as the emerging of the I, as described above in the case of primitive man. "In the beginning is relation as category of being, as readiness, as form that takes hold, as model for the soul. It is the *a priori* of relation, the *inborn Thou*" (31).

2. The Inborn Thou [78–79]

"The living relations are the realizations of the inborn Thou through the one that is met" (31). This Thou that is met is grasped as an opposite, apprehended in exclusiveness and addressed by the primary word. This indicates the *a priori* of relation. The inborn Thou realizes itself in the drive for contact, first tactile and then also optic, with another being, expressing more and more clearly a mutuality which indicates tenderness. This inborn Thou also determines later the creative drive, the drive to establish things synthetically or, if that is not possible, analytically by decomposing and tearing apart, so that there ensues a personification of the product, a conversation between two beings, which is the I-Thou communication.

The child's development as a human being is the development of his desire for the Thou—the fulfilment and frustration of this desire, its experiments and perplexities. The phenomenon may be properly understood when it is observed and investigated in the light of its cosmic-metacosmic origin, namely, as a projection of the undifferentiated, not-yet-formed primal world. From this primal state emerges an individual that is physically born into the world, but that is not a fully embodied, actualized being until it has gradually disengaged itself from its primal state through entering-in-relation. The child, though physically separated from his metacosmic origin, is not yet a fully independent, exclusive being until he has entered into relation with another Thou. He has an inborn Thou, but it becomes an "other" only through his act of entering-in-relation. The child strives to realize his inborn Thou as that of an other, but cannot grasp it in his own being in actuality except insofar as he relates to an actual Thou, that is, an actual "other."

6. *Development of I-It Communication*

A. EMERGENCE OF THE CONSCIOUS I [80]

"Man becomes an I through the Thou" (32). In the coming and going of confrontation, as the relational events condense and dissipate, there emerges with ever growing clarity the consciousness of the constant partner, the I, at first in the web of relation to the Thou, cognizable as that which reaches out for the Thou, but is not it. There is an awareness that that which strives for the Thou is not the Thou, but neither is it yet the I, as such. Then it breaks through more forcefully until the connection of I-Thou is sprung and the released I confronts itself for a moment as a Thou, that is, the I-Thou is sprung into a duality in man himself. The I then takes hold of itself and, through the consciousness which comes from the moment of confronting itself, enters into a new communication of I-It. The I, loosened from the Thou, confronts the latter as its own inborn Thou, but soon becomes aware of itself as a conscious I in communication with an other. But that other is no longer a Thou but is now an It.

B. EMERGENCE OF IT [80–81]

The new combination of I-It can now take place. As the Thou fades out of the relation, it does not yet become an It to an I, that is, an object of experience, but in a way an *It-for-itself*, awaiting its rise in the new communicative event, in I-It. The physical being, as it ripened into a body, lifted itself out of its surroundings and became the bearer of the body's sensations and the propagator of its drives. This was still an orientation in the coexistence of I and It side by side, and not a complete separation of I from an object. But now, out of the substantial fulness of I-Thou, steps forth the transformed, separated I, shrunk to a functional point of experiencing and using objects, and directs itself toward the It-for-itself, takes possession of it, and places itself into the other primary word, in I-It. "The man who has become disposed as an I, who says I-It, places himself before the things, not over against them, in the stream of mutual action" (33). The I as subject cannot remain a separate existent over against the things, but must become their subject, as they become its objects, as an I to an It in the I-It communication. The I is not an existent without an It; both are now in the second way of communication, namely, of subject-object connection.

C. SPACE, TIME, AND CAUSALITY [81–82]

1. In an Ordered World of Subject-Object Connection (as in Physical Science)

Man who says I-It may observe things as objects under his magnifying glass or arrange them in scenic order through his field glass. He isolates them as objects without regard to their exclusiveness, or connects them without feeling their world import. "He now experiences the things as sums of properties" (33). These may be the same properties that revealed themselves as a whole in the Thou, but now they become properties of the things, in separation, in terms of dreams, images, concepts, according to each man's particular manner of speaking I-It. The properties are separated, singled out, classified, formulated into concepts and ideas—in a word, ordered into a system of cause and effect. Man now places the things in a spatio-temporal-causal connection. Each thing is assigned its place, time of expiration, size, and condition, in an ordered world.

2. In a World-Order of Subject-Subject Relation (between I and Thou)

The Thou, to be sure, also appears in space, but in

the sense of exclusive confrontation, leaving everything else from which it emerges in the background, but not as its boundary or measuring rod. Space means here exclusiveness as a keeping out of everything else from the particular encounter, which is always a unique act of relation. But this meaning of space is not one that sets a limit or boundary around the Thou which has to be overcome. The Thou is not limited by the act of relation. It is an exclusive being in mutuality.

The Thou appears also in time, but as a self-fulfilled occurrence. It is not a part of a steady, discrete succession, but rather a living moment whose purely intensive dimension is prescribed by it alone. Time means here a moment of living relation, an occurrence which does not repeat itself or succeed itself in a series of intervals. It is a happening.

The Thou appears simultaneously as affecting and being affected, but not as linked in a chain of causes. It is in mutual interaction with the I from the beginning to the end of the occurrence. One being affects the other in the relational event but does not cause its existence or action; neither one determines the other. In the relation one is neither a cause nor an effect. Although both beings are in mutuality, they are independent of each other in the causal sense.

"This is the basic truth of the human world, that only 'It' may be ordered. Things may be coordinated only when out of our Thou they become It. The Thou knows no system of coordination" (34). Only It may be ordered according to a given coordinate system, as, for example, the Cartesian or Einstein coordinates. But an ordered world is not the same as a world-order. The first is basically physicomathematical, according to

modern concepts of science; the latter is an order of
living relations. The relations may be present in moments of silence, but these moments yield no content of
physical things in systematic order. They are immortal
and most ephemeral, never repeating themselves, but
their force penertates creation and man's cognition.
Their rays pierce through the ordered world and scat-
ter it again and again. The living relations are manifest
in the physical world, break into its order, and seem
to disorganize it. "This is the history of the individual
as it is that of the species" (35).

7. *The Twofold World: Recapitulation* [82–85]

"To man the world is twofold, according to his twofold communication" (35).

A. THE ORDERED WORLD

In the world of I-It man perceives beings as things,
and occurrences and actions as events; things composed
of properties, and events of moments; things posited in
a spatial network, and moments in a temporal network;
things and events delimited, compared, and measured by
other things and events—in all, a circumscribed world.
This world is in some measure reliable; its order is predictable as cause and effect. It is your object and remains so at your pleasure. You experience it; you accept it as truth. "It allows itself to be accepted by you,
but does not give itself to you" (35). There is a distance between you and the world of things, which you
can never bridge. The separation of the I from the
Thou cannot be overcome in the world of I-It. This

world is a common object for all, and you can talk about it intelligently to others, in terms of concepts, ideas, measurable entities, or classified units, but you cannot meet others in it. "You cannot prevail in life without it; . . . but if you died within it, you would be buried in nothingness" (35–36).

B. THE WORLD-ORDER

In the world of I-Thou man meets being and becoming as his counterpart; each is an exclusive being in an exclusive occurrence. Without measure or comparison, each being is over against you to the extent that it has become actual in the meeting. "The meetings do not order themselves into a world, but each is a sign for you of a world-order" (36). This world-order appears to you always anew and is thus unpredictable and unreliable, for there is no cause-and-effect prediction in it. It reaches out to you even when not summoned. If it does not meet you, it disappears but returns in a different guise. It always calls on you to respond; if you fail to meet it, it comes again but not in the same relation as before, for each relational event is unique and is not repeatable.

You and this world-order give yourselves to each other, one saying Thou to the other, and that is your present, that is, "being there" to say Thou. You can make it your object of experience and use, but you must do so repeatedly, for there is no present then. When you make it an object, you are not there; you place yourself at a distance, separated in time and space. While you are in the I-Thou, you stand alone in this world, facing the Thou, unable to talk about it to others, outside the relation, for then the meeting would break. "But it teaches you to meet others and stand firm in the meeting. . . . It does not help to preserve you in life; it only helps you to gain a presentiment of the eternal" (37).

C. PREROGATIVE OF THE ORDERED WORLD [84–85]

"The world of It is interconnected in space and time; the world of Thou has no such interconnection" (37).

The world of It has these two basic privileges. After the lapse of the relational occurrence, the individual Thou *must* become an It; the individual It *can* become a Thou by entering a relational occurrence again. These two basic states prompt man to view the world of It as the one in which he has to live and in which it is possible to live—indeed, the one that offers all kinds of inducements and stimuli, activities and knowledge. The moments of Thou appear in this world of It as wonderful lyric-dramatic episodes, full of magic, but dangerously attacking its well-tested interconnections in space and time, shattering, questioning rather than confirming the sense of security. This world of It is called "our world" or generally "the world."

Since one must return from the moments of Thou to "the world," why not stay in it without venturing again into relation? Why not call the other which we encounter in I-Thou relation to order and bring it home as an object of "the world"? If one is unable to say Thou in truth to father, wife, associate, why not say it just the same and mean "It"? Furthermore, the sheer present of the I-Thou encounter is so consuming that it would be impossible to tarry in it even for a while if there were no provision for stepping out of it speedily. On the other hand, it is quite possible to live in the sheer past of the world of It; indeed, it is only there that an ordered life may be established, that is, a life of experiencing and using. Why then not stay in this ordered world? However, Buber declares, "in all earnestness of truth, hear this: without It a human being cannot live. But he who lives with It alone is not a human being" (38).

PART TWO:
The World of It

8. *Expansion of the World of It*

A. MAN'S GROWING CAPACITY OF EXPERIENCING AND USING [87–89]

The history of the individual and that of the human race indicate a progressive increase of the world of It. This is being questioned with reference to the history of the race. It is pointed out that each culture starts equally from a primitive structure and, thus, with a small world of objects. It is therefore the individual culture and not the human race as a whole that corresponds to the life of the individual. But on closer examination we find that a culture does not just increase its objective realm by itself, but also takes over an influx of preceding cultures either directly, as Greece incorporated contemporaneous Egyptian culture, or indirectly, as western Christianity absorbed the past Greek culture. Moreover, the comparison is in terms not only of the range of a knowledge of nature, but also of social differentiation and technical accomplishment, both of which extend the objective world.

"Man's primary connection with the world of It encompasses *experience*, which constitutes this world recurrently, and *using*, which provides for its manifold purpose of sustaining, alleviating, and equipping human life. As the range of the world of It increases, the capacity to experience and use it must also increase" (40). This capacity unavoidably develops from generation to generation even though the individual may also avail himself of acquired knowledge and specialization, that is, transmitted experiencing and using. This is what is usually meant by progress of spiritual life, which, however, is a sin in words committed against the spirit, because the expansion of experiencing and using is a diminution of man's power of relation, whereby alone man may live in spirit.

B. LIFE IN SPIRIT AND IN THINGS [89–90]

"Spirit, in its human revelation, is the response of man to his Thou" (41). Whether man speaks through language, art, or action, the spirit is the same, namely, the response to the Thou which appears and addresses itself out of the mystery. "Spirit is word." The speaking may form itself in words in the human brain and become audible through the throat; in truth, however, language is not in man, but man stands in language and speaks out of it. All that is word is spirit. "Spirit is not in the I but between the I and Thou. It is not like the blood that circulates in you, but like the air in which you breathe" (41). When man is able to respond to the Thou, he lives in spirit; and he is able to do it only by virtue of his power of relation. Spirit is created between I and Thou when man enters-in-relation with the Thou. Spirit is the between or the relation.

"All response engages (*bindet*) the Thou in the world of It. This is man's melancholy, and this is his greatness" (42). This is the destiny of the relational event. The more powerful the response, the more it restrains the Thou, forcing it to turn into an object. Only silence toward the Thou, the reserved abiding in the unformed, unarticulated word, leaves the Thou free so that man may stand in the relationship where the spirit *is*, though it does not become manifest. When man enters-in-relation with the Thou, spirit comes into existence. As long as he abides in it, the spirit is there, though not manifested in a given form. But when he articulates his response to the Thou, he thereby forces it to become an It. The stronger the articulation, the greater is the force which banishes the Thou from the relational occurrence into the objective world. That is how there comes to be cognition, a work, an image, and a symbol in the midst of the living. But what has thus been transformed into an It, into a thing, is also destined to flame up again into a present and to return to the element from which it came, to the Thou, once more to be confronted by man in a living present. This was intended in the original confrontation when spirit first elicited the response. If man is satisfied only with experiencing and using the world of It, he thwarts the meaning of this destiny. Instead of freeing the It, he holds it down; instead of looking, he observes it; instead of accepting, he evaluates it.

C. THE WORLD OF IT IN KNOWLEDGE, ART, AND ACTION [90–92]

1. In Knowledge Being unlocks itself to knowledge when man looks at that which confronts him pres ently (*gegenwärtiglich*). But he will of necessity grasp it as an object (*Gegenstand*), compare it with other objects, arrange them in order, describe them, and analyze them, for being can enter conceptual knowledge only as an It. "But in the seeing, it was not a thing among things or an event among events, but exclusively present (*gegenwärtig*)" (43) Being communicates *itself* and not the *law* abstracting from its appearance. What is conceived as universal is only an "unrolling" of a cluster-like occurrence which was seen as a particular in the relational event, and which is now contained in the form of It in conceptual knowledge. One may view a general concept as the unraveling of that which was seen as a particular being in the relational occurrence. That is, knowledge of things in general concepts leads to a knowledge that the things have been converted from particular, exclusive beings which confronted man in living relations. But one can also engage knowledge so as to let what has become an It remain just a thing to be experienced and used, and to be applied for the investigation of the world and thus for its conquest.

2. In Art Form unlocks itself to the artist when he looks at that which confronts him. The image is not in a world of gods but in this very world of men. It is here, only it is dormant even when the human eye searches it out. It longs like a dream to meet with men who will lift the ban and embrace the form even for a timeless event. Man experiences how it is made, what it expresses, its qualities and rank. To be sure, scientific and esthetic understanding are necessary in order for man to do his work faithfully and delve into the truth of relation, which is beyond the understandable yet embraces it.

3. In Pure Action Action, which is not self-willed, leads man even higher toward the star of spirit than in the case of cognition and art. For here, transitory, corporeal man depends not on images of stable matter but on himself as the more abiding image of pure action without arbitrary wilfulness. "Here the Thou appeared to man from the deepest mystery, addressed him directly from the darkness, and he responded with his life" (44). Here the word has often become life, which is teaching, whether it fulfils the law or breaks it. "At times both are needed in order that the spirit may not die on earth" (44). What is thus taught to succeeding generations is not what is or what ought to be, "but how one may live in spirit, in the face of Thou." This means that the world of Thou which always touches the coming generations is to be opened to them. But those who have become displeased with the living encounter profess a different teaching. "They have confined the person to history and its talk to books. They have codified the fulfilment, as well as the breaking, of the law" (45).

Pure action which stems from spirit reveals the original relational event more truly than in the case of knowledge and art. It is life itself and should be taught to the succeeding generations as a living model of the encounter with reality in spirit. But what happens with people who have no patience with life in the encounter is that they congeal these actions in history books and codified laws, like a living finger in a dead skull.

9. *Development of the Function of Experiencing and Using* [92–95]

"The development of the function of experiencing

and using is attained mostly through a reduction of man's power of relation" (45). He who wants to use the spirit as a means of gratification separates the I from the It and divides his life with fellowmen into two regions: (1) the region of It or the establishments, and (2) the region of I or feelings. The first is the "outer" range, in which this man works, deals, organizes, preaches, and sets himself all kinds of goals. It is the coordinated structure within which many human brains and brawns perform their daily affairs. The second is the "inner" domain, in which he lives and recuperates from his toils in the establishments. Here he feels at home, enjoys his likes and hates, pleasures and even pains, if they are not too severe. "The establishments are a complicated market place; the feelings are a boudoir rich in constant diversities. The boundary between the two regions is always imperiled as the mischievous feelings sometimes break into the most practical establishments. But with some good will, it may be restored" (46). It is most difficult to rely on this boundary in the regions of so-called personal life. In married life it is not easily delineated but is manageable. In so-called public life it is perfectly drawn, as witness the heaven-storming conventions of parties and movements in contrast to their everyday business-like machinery. "But the separated It of the establishments is a *golem*, and the separated I of the feelings is a soul-bird fluttering about" (46). The one knows man only as a specimen, the other only as an object, but neither knows him as a person in mutuality. The one knows only the sheer past, that which is already over; the other knows only the flitting moment, that which is not yet. But neither knows the present, and neither has an approach to real life. "Establishments yield no public life, and feelings no personal life" (46). The first condition has been generally recognized and is the source of the searching distress of our age. The second has been understood by only a few, and the more modern man busies himself with his feelings, the more he despairs of this unreality. Yet he learns nothing from his despair, because he finds that too is an interesting feeling.

People who suffer from the fact that establishments do not yield public life hit upon the device of saving these establishments through "freedom of feeling." Thus the automated state tries to substitute a community of love for real mutuality among its citizens, who are essentially strangers to each other. This community of love is supposed to arise if the people live together with free "boundless feelings" toward each other. "But this is not so. The true community does not arise from feelings which people may have for each other—much as it cannot be without them—but through these two things: that they all stand in living mutual relation with a living center, and that they stand in living mutual relation between themselves" (47). These relations include feelings but are not derived from them. The community builds itself up through a mutuality of relation but it is the living Center that is the master-builder (This concept will be developed in Section 35a. The Center, which Buber has in mind is the Absolute Thou or God. The persons who direct themselves to the Absolute Thou are the bearers of communality, which is the principle of community-forming.)

Neither can the establishments of so-called personal life be renewed through "free feelings," much as the cannot be without them. Marriage will never renew itself except through its true origin, namely, "that two persons reveal their Thou to each other. Out of this a marriage is built by the Thou, which is neither of the I's. This is the metaphysical and metapsychical factor of love, which is only accompanied by the feeling of love" (48). Any other attempt to renew marriage is a denial of this factor. In fact, if one discounted from the much publicized erotic of our age everything that has to do with the I, that is, what pertains to one's own pleasure, nothing else would be left. "True public life and true personal life are two forms of a union (*Verbundenheit*)." Feelings or the changing content, and establishment or the constant form, are necessary so that content and form may combine and abide, but they do not create human life. What creates it is the third element, the central presentness of the Thou—more truly speaking, "the central Thou that is addressed in the present" (48). (This idea will be treated more fully in Part Three.)

10. *Good and Evil*

A. THE WORLD OF IT IS NOT EVIL [95–96]

"The primary word I-It is not evil—as matter is not evil. It is of evil like the matter which presumes to be the present being (*das Seiende*)" (49). One who allows this to happen is choked up by the world of It, and his own I is depersonalized "until the demon over him and the phantom within him whisper to one another the admission of their being fettered" (49).

But is not the communal life of modern man of necessity sunk in the world of It? It seems that the economy and the state, the two compartments of this life, can have no other ground than one that forgoes all immediacy, which is alien to them. The dominant functions of the economy and the state are experiencing and using, out of which the great establishments have been built up and maintained. Statesmen and economists depend for their success on their dealings with people as objects fulfilling set goals and not as bearers of Thou, which cannot be used. Their world would collapse if instead of computing many He's into one It they summed up many Thou's, which would yield just another Thou. This would mean replacing reason with fuzzy, amateurish dreams. Apart from that, it would destroy the precision apparatus of our civilization, which alone makes life of the ever-increasing masses possible. Such is the argument of those who are sunk in the world of It.

But those who advance this argument hardly believe it themselves, for they know that the leaders no longer direct the state but rather service a machine rushing in madness. And the masters of industry, though claiming that they adjust the apparatus to the conditions, really adjust themselves to the apparatus, that is, as long as it permits them to do so. Their spokesmen assure you that the economy is the inheritance of the state. "But you know that there is nothing to inherit but the tyranny of this exorbitantly profitable It, under which the I, growing ever more powerless to control, still dreams that it is in command" (50–51).

B. GOOD IS DIRECTION TOWARD RELATION [96–100]

"The communal life of man can no more than man

himself dispense with the world of It, as the response of Thou hovers over it like the spirit over the waters" (51). Man's will to profit and power has a natural and proper effect as long as it is linked with his will to enter-in-relation. No impulse is evil until it breaks away from being. The impulse that is linked with and determined by being is the plasma of communal life; the separated impulse destroys it. The economy or will to profit, and the state or will to power, partake of life as long as they are part of the spirit. Just introducing any kind of immediacy will not help. The loosening of the economy or state will not compensate for the fact that it is no longer governed by the spirit which says Thou. "No stirring up of the periphery will substitute for the living relation with the Center." Communal life is sustained by the power of relation which penetrates its members.

The statesman or economist who is subject to the spirit is not an amateur. He knows that he cannot confront the people he deals with simply as bearers of the Thou, without breaking up his work. Yet he risks this to the limit set by the spirit. He is not a dreamer, but serves the truth without rejecting reason. "He does in communal life nothing but what is done in personal life by a man who knows that he is unable to realize the Thou in its purity and yet confirms it daily with the It, within the reason and measure of the day, drawing the limit anew each day—discovering the limit" (52). Man is not expected to do more than he can within the limitations of his operations in the world of It, provided that he allows himself to be guided by the spirit of the I-Thou relation which permeates his actions. The limits of his actions are to be set by the spirit, not just by the

It. Thus labor and ownership can also be redeemed only through the persence of the spirit, so that what is produced and possessed, while remaining attached to the world of It, may become transfigured as the confronting other, as a representation of the Thou. There is no turning back from modern technological advancements, but there is an anticipated going beyond and out.

If the state and the economy are not transformed, it does not matter which regulates the other. It is important that the establishment of the state become freer and that of the economy more just, but this is not the problem which is posed before life, since they certainly cannot become so out of their own accord. What is decisive is whether the spirit, which can say Thou, is active in reality, whether it affects communal life independently and is not subject to state and economy just to suit their expediency, whether the spirit in man's personal life is embodied in his communal life. This cannot be achieved by a division of the latter into independent regions, one of which is "the spiritual life." That would leave the area in the world of It entirely to the rule of tyranny and would also completely deprive the spirit of reality. For the spirit does not act in life as an independent entity, but affects the world, its power penetrating the realm of It. The spirit is truly "at its own" when it confronts the closed-off world, gives itself over to this world, and redeems it and thereby itself. The weakened, contradictory spirituality that in our day is taken for the spirit could not do this unless it returned to the essence of spirit, that is, was able to say Thou. By separating a spiritual life from the actual daily affairs of the state and the economy, we create a make-believe spirituality, devoid of any power to influence our life.

11. *Causality and Freedom*

A. CAUSALITY AND DECISION [100–101]

"Causality reigns in the world of It without restraint" (53). Every experienced physical or psychic event is of necessity taken as causing and being caused. This includes also events in the continuum of It to which we may attribute purpose as an end in view or final cause. Teleology is part of causality set in reverse but the order is not disrupted. The action in teleology is determined by the end, which is an anticipated cause, or a motive for the action. Man does not feel oppressed by this rule of causality, which is important in the scientific order of nature, if he is not confined within the world of It, but brings it back constantly into the world of relation. Man sees the world in causal connection in order to explain its operation, but he is aware of the fact that in real living experience the connection is of an immediate relation between beings neither of which causes the other. (See Section 6c.) Here I and Thou stand freely opposite each other in mutual effect but not drawn into causality. Here freedom is assured to both man and Being. Only one who knows relation and is aware of the presence of Thou is capable of decision and is thus free. Buber views the act of decision as the act of freedom. Man is able to decide only if he is not determined by the one which confronts him—in other words, when he stands in relation and not in causal connection. This is explained as follows:

Before man has formed his world, it stands before him in all its potencies and in great agitation as a temptation for good or evil. The moment he feels gripped by a hidden hand that demands his act of being to enter-in-relation, there emerge two—the task and the illusion. Man has to choose. At that moment realization begins; man comes to a decision to act, that is, he chooses the task. But he does not leave out the other, the illusion, but turns its force into the very act of his choosing, in the performance of the task. He chooses to realize the good. This is decision, freedom. But he does not exclude evil altogether but converts it into a force for the good. Man decides the occurrence when he draws the passion of the not-chosen into the realization of the chosen, that is, even when he "serves God with the evil inclination." Man does not really choose evil, but draws its passion into the act of carrying out the task, which is good. Thus he serves God when he does good even (or especially) with the passion of his evil inclination. Evil means here the passion which can cause harm when left undirected, but which can be turned into good through direction. According to Buber, direction can be only toward God; otherwise it is not direction but going astray. This is the meaning of the heading of Section 10b, "Good is Direction toward Relation." In Buber's view, man is neither good nor evil but can do evil when he loses direction, that is, goes astray. Properly understood, what is called the upright is that which is addressed, that toward which one directs himself and decides. "And if there were a devil, it would not be the one who decided against God, but who, unto eternity, did not decide" (55).

B. FREEDOM IS DESTINY [101–103]

"Causality does not oppress the man who is assured of freedom. He knows that his mortal life, in its very being, is a swinging between Thou and It, and he senses its meaning" (55). He cannot tarry in the relation, but it is enough for him that he can step on its threshold repeatedly, for it is the very meaning and destiny of his life that he must leave it repeatedly. There, on the threshold, the response, the spirit, rekindles itself, but its spark must stand the test here, in the world of It. "What is here called necessity cannot frighten him, for over here he recognized true necessity—destiny" (55). His destiny to step in and out of relation is what makes him human and enables him to bring the spark of the spirit into everyday living in the world of things.

The mystery reveals itself in the discovery of the deed which is intended for me, and also in its resistance to my carrying it out as I intended. My discovery and decision, as well as my failure to carry out the task fully, are all my destiny, which does not impair my freedom, for that *is* my freedom. One who forgets causality and decides out of the depth of the encounter with the Thou is a free man who meets destiny. Freedom and destiny are counterparts in the relation. Destiny is not man's boundary but his fulfilment. Freedom and destiny are interwoven in the meaning in which destiny looks on like grace itself.

In sum, it is man's destiny, as a category of being who relates to other beings, of necessity to encounter the other. But it is his freedom to respond, and if he does respond, he fulfils his destiny freely by meeting the other in the I-Thou relation. This makes him a

human being. Thus his destiny is his fulfilment just as
his free response is his fulfilment, both meaning the
same thing—his human completion. If he fails to respond to the encounter, he can only experience and use
the other as an It, and he becomes aware of himself
as an experiencing I, a subject having an object. But
then he is not the human being that he is destined to
become. He who fulfils his destiny in relation, fulfils
himself as man in the world of It.

"No, the man who carries the spark as he returns
to the world of It is not weighed down by causal necessity" (56). In times of healthy life, confidence flows
from men of spirit to the masses. Everybody, even the
dullest, has somehow naturally, faintly encountered the
presence; all have somewhere been aware of the Thou.
They are assured of the spirit. But when the times are
sick, the world of It is no longer fructified by the living
stream of the world of Thou, and, thus separated, the
It overwhelms man like a ghost of the swamps. He
succumbs to the world of objects which are no longer
rendered present. "Then familiar causality builds itself
up to an oppressive, crushing fate" (56).

12. *Culture: Destiny or Fate* [103–105]

"Every great culture which embraces many nations
rests on a primal event of meeting, on a response to
the Thou that took place at its source, on an act of
being by the spirit" (56). Strengthened in the same
direction by the force of succeeding generations, it
produces in spirit a particular conception of the cosmos
through which man's cosmos of everyday life becomes
possible. In a particular spatial orientation man may

then build houses for himself and for God, fill the time with songs, and form human society. But man remains free and creative only so long as he possesses the original act of being and can enter-in-relation. If his culture ceases to center in the living, renewed relational event, it congeals into the world of It and may only occasionally be broken through by the deeds of solitary spirits. Causality, which heretofore was unable to disturb the spiritual orientation in the cosmos, now becomes an oppressive, crushing fate. Destiny, which gave meaning to the cosmos and ruled over causality, has turned into a meaningless demon. The same Karma which our ancestors regarded as propitious for raising them to a future life in higher spheres is considered by us as tyranny, for the deed of previous unknown life threw us in prison from which we cannot escape in this life. Once, we needed only to accept Dike, whose heavenly "way" also meant our way, in order to dwell with a free heart within the bounds of necessity. Now Heimarmene, a stranger to the spirit, weighs us down with every one of our deeds.

In Greek religion, Dike was the goddess of justice, whose function was to harmonize the conflicts between nature and moral conduct. Heimarmene was the blind force of nature that knows no moral law. One could appeal to Dike and adjust one's ways to her rule of justice. But Heimarmene was blind, relentless fate which did not heed man's supplication. No redemption was possible under her sway. The yearning for redemption would remain unsatisfied until one might learn to escape the wheel of births, or until someone might save the lost souls unto the children of God.

"The sickness of our age is unlike that of other ages,

but it is part of them all" (58). The history of culture is not like a race in which every runner must cover the same death-round. Cultures do not progress in a straight line, but rise and fall in a spiral, going down to the depths of the spiritual underground, which may be called also an ascent to an innermost whirl from which there is no going forward or backward—only a *return*. The "return" does not mean starting over again from the beginnings of the culture's origin, but rather returning to the right path from which it went astray. But must we go on this spiraling whirls to the end, before we realize the danger? "Where there is danger, rescue too grows" (58).

A. BELIEF IN FATE UNDER DISGUISE
[105–107]

"The quasi-biological and quasi-historical thinking of today, however different one may appear from the other, has contrived to establish a belief in fate more tenacious and oppressive than any that has ever existed" (58). It is no longer Karma or the power of stars that governs the fate of man, but many forces which most of our contemporaries believe to be a mixture of those powers, much like the mixture of gods in which the late Romans believed. This is alleviated by various claims, be it the "law of life" of a universal struggle in which everyone must fight along or perish, or the "law of a soul" that constructs a psychical person entirely out of a complex of inborn drives, or the "social law" of an irresistible social process of which the will and consciousness are only adjuncts, or the "cultural law" of historical forms that come into being and disappear in an unchangeable uniform manner, and various other "laws"—the claim "always means that man is framed within an inescapable occurrence against which he cannot defend himself or may do so only in his madness" (59)

In ancient beliefs in fate there was the possibility of gaining freedom from the power of the stars through initiation into their mysteries. Similarly, Brahman-offerings promised redemption from the force of Karma. But now the mixture-idols tolerate no salvation and no belief in redemption. Freedom from determinate forces of the laws of nature is regarded as sheer folly. The alternatives are "a determinate slavery or a hopelessly rebellious one" (59). Notwithstanding the talk about teleological development and organized emergence, it is all grounded in limitless causality. The dogmas of process leave no room for freedom, that is, for the power to return which changes life on earth. Process does not know man, who overcomes the universal struggle and rejuvenates the historical structure through return. Its dogmas allow only the inevitable in life; "freedom" is relegated to one's soul. "But the one who returns deems such freedom as the most abject slavery" (59). "Return" here signifies a complete break with one's wayward conduct in personal as well as public life; it denotes not a turning back to some former existence, but a turning away from the conduct which knows only the It, and a turning toward the Thou, the other, in reality, the "other" meaning God as well as man.

"The only thing that can become fateful to man is belief in fate" (60). Such belief holds back the movement for a return. It is a false belief, to begin with. The process, as such, is only an arrangement of becoming in a certain order, as if the detached units thus arranged were history. It has no access to the presence of the Thou; it does not know the reality of the spirit. One who is overwhelmed by the world of It is bound to see in the dogmas of process, as understood in the physical and biological sciences, for example, the creation of untarnished truth. Actually, this only puts man more deeply in bondage to the world of It. But one who can return in this world with the power of entering-in-relation will become aware of real freedom. "And to become free is to free oneself from the belief in nonfreedom" (60–61).

B. WILL, NOT WILFULNESS [107–111]

Many may learn to gain the upper hand over the world of It, as one overcomes the power of a demon, by calling it by its real name and recognizing its essence, namely, that it is the isolation and alienation of that from which every earthly Thou arises. "How can there arise in a being the buried power of entering-in-relation, when the nimble hobgoblin keeps heaping wreckage over it? How can one who lives in wilfulness gain an inner awareness of freedom" (61)? Can one who possesses the phantom, who is a depersonalized I, bring himself to call the demon by name?

As freedom and destiny belong together, so do wilfulness and fate. But, whereas the former pair give each other meaning, the latter avoid one another in a meaninglessness which is manifest only as nonfreedom. "The free man is one who wills without wilfulness. He believes in reality, that is, in the real tie between the real duality of I and Thou." He believes that determination needs him and that he must go out toward it, though he does not know where it stands. But he knows that he must go out with his whole being. "It will not come exactly as intended by his decision, but what will come, will come only when he decides on that which he is able to will" (62). He does not attack, nor does he just let the encounter happen. What he meets comes out of the way of being in the world. He listens to it and realizes it as it wants to be realized through human life and death. To believe means here to meet. (The meaning of belief or faith in the act of meeting will be discussed in Sections 34 and 35.)

"Wilful man does not believe and does not meet" (62). He does not know the inner connection; he only knows the outer world and his passion to use it. Even when he speaks of his determination and says Thou, he means "Thou which I can use," as he himself is determined by things and drives which he carries out wilfully. He has no "grand will" but a determination of drives. He is incapable of sacrifice, is never concrete. He has a design but just "lets it happen," claiming to help it by such means as *its* determination calls for, not *his* determination. He follows what he regards as the course of nature through technological means. This to him is freedom: that he can use technology as he pleases, according to design.

"But the free man does not have a design for which he then adduces the means. He has only one thing—his decision always to reach his determination." He may have to renew it occasionally when he finds himself at the crossroads, but he never loses faith that "the direction of the grand will" is sufficient unto itself without mediation. The "grand will" is manifest in the relation of man with the Absolute Thou or God. (This is

discussed in Part Three.) On the other hand, the dis-
believing, wilful man knows only disbelief and wilfulness, only the contriving of designs and means. His
world is called *fate*. Thus the wilful man is entangled
in nonreality. He knows this, and he uses his spiritual
efforts to *disguise* his thoughts. None the less, the knowledge that his world is not real, his reflection on the unreal I and the real I which is his despair, leading to self-
destruction and rebirth, "could be the beginning of the
return" (63–64).

13. *The Person and the Individual*

A. THE I AND SELF-CONSCIOUSNESS
[111–115]

Granted that the world of It, if left to itself without
contact with the Thou, will turn into an estranged
demon, how is it that the I becomes unreal? The I is
secure in its self-consciousness, whether it lives in relation or outside of it. "I see Thee" and "I see a tree"
may not have the same actuality in seeing, but they both
have the same actual I. This seems to be the case, but
upon investigation we find that it is not so. The word-
form proves nothing. The Thou may often mean It and
vice versa. Similarly, the I may just stand as a pronoun
for "this one who speaks." But if the Thou and the I
are meant to stand for relation in the one and experience in the other, then the self-conscious I spoken in
each is not the same. (See Section 2, "Experience and
Relation.") "The I of the primary word I-It appears as
a self-existent individual (*Eigenwesen*) and becomes
conscious of itself as a subject [of experiencing and
using]. The I of the primary word I-Thou appears as

a person and becomes conscious of itself as a subjectivity [without a dependent genitive]." An individual is a *separation* from other individuals. A person is one who *enters-in-relation* with other persons. The one breaks away; the other seeks inner connection. The one lives and dies through experiencing and using; the other aims to realize its own being in its eternal essence through contact with the Thou, "for through the contact with every Thou a breath of eternal life touches us" (65). (The relation of each Thou to the eternal Thou is developed in Part Three, Sections 15 ff.)

Reality is participation without appropriation, and it is the more complete the more the contact with the Thou is immediate. Thus the I is made real to the extent that participation is made complete. Yet the I which steps out of the relational event into separation and self-consciousness does not lose its reality. Participation is preserved in it in its living potency, and that is the *domain of subjectivity*, in which the I is aware of its inner connection and separation in one. "Genuine subjectivity can be understood only dynamically, as the swinging of the I in its solitary truth. Here is also the place where the desire is formed and heightened for ever higher, more unconditioned relation, for more complete participation in being. In subjectivity the spiritual substance of the person ripens" (66). The person becomes conscious of himself as participant in being, as coexistent, and thus as a being. The self-existent individual becomes conscious of himself as being-so-and-none-other. "The person says 'I am'; the individual, 'this I am.' 'Know thyself' means for the person 'know thee as being'; for the individual it means 'know your being-thus.' By his very separation from others, the individual sets himself at a distance from being" (66). Buber distinguishes between two primary acts of man: (a) distancing that sets the world apart from the human being and then connects the two through mediation between subject and object, and (b) relation between man and the world as subject-subject without mediation.

The above distinction between person and individual means not that the person gives up his particular distinct being, but only that this is not his point of orientation when he is in the act of relation. The particularity of the individual, moreover, is an abstraction which he invented when he set himself up as the subject outside an object. His self is mostly known to him as a self-appearance capable of valuation, but also of deceiving itself in the process of valuating and other actions. To truly recognize the fiction of his own particularity, of being-thus, would lead him to self-destruction or rebirth, for his particularity has no present, only a past, like all things in the world of It. "The person beholds the self; the individual is preoccupied with 'mine': my kind, my race, my creation, my genius" (67). The individual does not take part in reality but tries to appropriate it as much as possible through experiencing and using. This is the dynamics of separating, *distancing*, and possessing the world of things. It is unreal because it does not grow into a substance but remains nothing but a subjective functional point. It is a subjective I inasmuch as it uses others, but is not a being who is *with* others.

"Not two kinds of human being are there, but two poles of humanity. No man is pure person and none pure individual; no one wholly real or wholly unreal.

Everyone lives in the twofold I" (67). But there are those who live primarily as persons, and others as individuals. Between them runs the course of true history. The more man or mankind is dominated by individual self-existence, the more the I degenerates into unreality, and the person in man and in humanity then leads a hidden, underground existence, until it is called upon to return.

B. THE PERSON IN RELATION TO MAN, NATURE, AND GOD [115–117]

"Man is the more of a person the stronger his humanly twofold I is of the primary word I-Thou." The way he speaks and means I determines his course. "The word I is the true shibboleth of mankind" (68). It sounds false when spoken with self-contradiction. One who speaks the separated I with a large capital shames the world-spirit as it becomes degraded into spirituality. (See Section 10b on spirituality as a degradation of the spirit.) We may take the living, emphatic I spoken by Socrates, for example, as an expression of faith in man's reality, standing by it even in solitude; or the full I spoken by Goethe in his pure "consort with nature," which reveals to him its secrets without betraying its mystery. For nature reveals itself in each relational event, as a particular occurrence, but not the mystery of the whole of nature. The spoken word of Jesus, to take another example, is overwhelming and self-evident. It is the I of unconditional relation, such that he who addresses himself to the Father can only be the son. His I means the holy word of the unconditional. (Buber regarded Jesus as a man who had attained the highest possible state of relation to God. The entire subject of

man's encounter with God is treated in Part Three).
Even if the I spoken by Jesus is touched by separation,
he still addresses the other out of his inner connection,
which remains the stronger of the two. This I cannot be
shrunk to a power in itself; nor can the Thou be reduced to something indwelling in man, which again
would render the presentness of relation unreal. "I and
Thou remain; everyone can speak Thou and is then I,
everyone can say father and is then son; reality abides"
(70).

C. THE I THAT IS AN IT [117–119]

But what about the man whose mission demands of
him that for the sake of his cause there be no relation
with a Thou but that everything and everyone become
an It subservient to the cause? What about Napoleon's
saying I,—is it not legitimate? "Is this phenomenon of
experiencing and using not a person" (70)? No, for
Napoleon, in fact, did not know the dimension of the
Thou. As said of him, every being had to have a value
for him. After his fall he compared those who denied
him with Peter, but he himself had no one he could
deny, for he recognized no one as a being. He was the
demoniac Thou of the millions that answers the Thou
with an It, that responds only with his own deeds. It is
"the demoniac Thou to whom no one can become a
Thou." This is the *third kind*, which is besides the person and the individual, not between them. He appears
in time of destiny. There are a thousandfold relations
to him, but none issues from him. All intend to participate in him as in reality, but he himself participates
in none. He sees all beings, including himself, only as
motor-capacities to his cause. He treats himself too as

an It. Thus the I he speaks is not a living I, yet his speaking is not to all appearances deceiving. He does not speak of himself but out of himself. "The I that he speaks and writes is the necessary subject of the sentence of his assertions and commands, no more and no less." It has no subjectivity, but also has no self-consciousness of being-thus, no self-appearance. When Napoleon was overthrown and could reflect about his I, he spoke of himself as "the clock that is there but does not know itself" (71). What appeared then as I was neither subject nor subjectivity; its enchantment was broken but not redeemed. It could say only "The All beholds us," and in the end sink back into mystery.

Who can say that after such a demise Napoleon understood or misunderstood his monstrous mission? However, it is certain that the age of which the demoniac becomes lord and symbol misunderstands it. What rules here is not lust for power, as such, but the execution of a fateful decree. Such an age is carried away by the commanding force of the face, not realizing that it is only "the face of the clock." The word I becomes a shibboleth. Napoleon spoke it, not in relation but as an execution, an impersonal I which executes the decree of fate. It only betrays a wickedness, one's self-contradiction.

14. *Alienation*

A. REFLECTION AND CONTRADICTION
[119–120]

What is self-contradiction? When man does not realize his inborn Thou in relation to the world, does not respond to the actual other, his Thou recoils inward.

It unfolds itself toward an impossible object of the I, that is, where no unfolding is possible. The inborn Thou cannot unfold as an object, only as a Thou other than itself, that is, as an actual other. Otherwise there ensues a confrontation within onself, which is not a relation or interaction between an I and a real other, but only a self-contradiction. If the *a priori* of relation does not realize itself in meeting an actual other in the world, then the inborn Thou, which is the bearer of this *a priori*, retreats toward the inner self and becomes an object to its own I. The confrontation is thus between an I and its object within man himself. The inborn Thou, instead of unfolding itself toward the actual Thou of another being, is reflected in the I and taken to be the other. This results in self-contradiction between the I and the inborn Thou taken as its object. Hence there is only a resemblance of relation, or an escape from the fulfilment of the *a priori* of relation with the world. This is man's *alienation from the world*. (See Section 5b on the *a priori* relation of the inborn Thou.)

B. TREMBLING AT ALIENATION [120–122]

At times, when man trembles at the alienation between the I and the world, he thinks something must be done about it. He is like a man in a dream, facing an abyss, seeing a possibility of getting across to life but not knowing the direction. He might perhaps find direction in inner knowledge of return by way of sacrifice, but he rejects this in preference to a thought-process in which he has greater confidence. The art of thinking, he feels, can give him a more credible and more familiar world-picture. Man therefore calls upon this rational artist to paint for him a picture, or rather two pictures on opposite walls. One, which moves before him like a cinema, is the *Universe* with little man standing on the tiny globe, carried along through history and always trying to reconstruct the anthill of civilization which history has trampled down. The inscription under this picture is "One and All."

On the other wall there is a picture of the *Soul*. A spinner spins, and the sphere of all the stars, the lives of all creatures, and the entire history of the world are no longer called by their names. Instead, all are woven out of one and the same thread and are termed sensations and presentations or even experiences of the psychic states. The inscription under this picture, too, is "One and All."

When man now happens to tremble at his alienation and *the world frightens him*, he looks up and chances upon one of the pictures: let it be the Universe. There he sees that the I is embedded in the world and that there really is no I, as such, and therefore he cannot be harmed by the world. And he is pacified. Or he looks up at the opposite picture and sees that the world is embedded in the I and that there really is no world, as such, and therefore he cannot be harmed by it. And he is pacified.

Another time, when man shudders at his alienation and *the I frightens him*, he looks at either picture and sees in the one that the I is submerged in the world, and he feels pacified; or he sees in the other picture that the world is stuffed into the empty I, and he is pacified. The I which frightened him is thus accounted for by the world without self-contradiction, as long as he does not see the other picture; or the world is ac-

unted for by the I without self-contradiction if he
sees only the Soul picture of the I. "But there comes a
time," says Buber, "and that is nigh, and trembling man
looks up and in a flash sees both pictures together. And
he is gripped by a deeper trembling" (75).

PART THREE:

Man's Encounter with God*

I. The I in Relation with the Eternal Thou

15. *The Complete Act of Meeting* [123–124]   God cannot become It

"The extended lines of relation intersect in the eternal Thou" (76). Through each particular Thou the
primary word speaks to the eternal, from which comes
fulfilment to all being. The inborn Thou becomes real
in the meeting with any other Thou, but completes itself only in the immediate relation with the One which
cannot become It. The way to the Eternal Thou or
God is the same as the way to man, except that the

*In order to present more clearly the nature of man's
relation to God in Buber's description of the encounter, the
whole Third Part is divided into five sections (I to V), each
subheading designating a certain aspect of the relation.

latter is never complete; the act of relation between man and man is never fully realized.

All the different names that man in the past gave the eternal Thou spoke not only *of* God but also *to* Him, even though the names were in the language of It. All of God's names are therefore hallowed, as they all speak to Him. Buber was once asked, "Why use the name God which has been much misused?" There is no need to abandon the use of the word God, he said, even though it has certainly been greatly misused. Indeed, it is the most tattered, yet most imperishable, word. Everyone who speaks to God means Him, because when man says the word God and really has Thou in mind he speaks to the true Thou of his own life, a Thou which cannot be confined by any other, →? divine and which includes all others. And he who detests the name and fancies himself to be godless, when he addresses with his whole being the Thou of his life, which cannot be confined by others, speaks to God.

16. *Two Parts of the Way* [124–126]

When we, on our way, meet a man who encounters us going his way, we know only our part of the way in the encounter, not his. Of his part we have only a lived experience (*Erlebnis*) in the meeting. Similarly, of the complete relational event in the encounter with God we know our stretch of the way, our going forth. The other part we know not; it happens upon us in the meeting. But we overreach ourselves if we talk of it as something which is beyond the meeting, in the sense of a separation, a barrier, or a stretch lying between us and the other, outside the meeting. Our concern here is not the other side but our side of the path; not the grace of God to man, but the will of man to meet Him. "The grace concerns us only in so far as we go forth toward it and await its presence; it is not our object" (77). For we seek not to attain the other as an object of our possession or understanding but only to go out on our way to the encounter. The Thou confronts me, and I step into immediate relation with it. Thus the relation is my choosing and being chosen, active and passive in one. Activity of the whole being, as a suspension of all partial activities and their sensations, must become the same as passivity. In the relation, which is mutuality, I am active as a whole and at the same time passive as a whole. "This is the activity of man, who has become a whole, which is called not-doing, in which man is not agitated by anything of a particular partial nature, that is, nothing in him seizes upon the world." He does not seize the world through any particular faculty, such as understanding or feeling in itself, but relates with his being as a whole. "Here the whole man is affected in his complete, reposing wholeness; here man has become an operative whole" and not one who operates through a single faculty. "To have constancy in this condition means to be able to go forth toward the highest meeting" (78).

This does not call for the abandonment of the world of sensation as illusion. There is no world that is an illusion; there is only the world that appears to us twofold, according to our twofold communication with it. We need only do away with the notion that there is a sensate world separate from a real world, or with the idea that we must transcend sensate experience in order to reach the real world. Every experience, even the spiritual one, as distinguished from living relation, can produce only an It, an object of material or spiritual possession and use. Nor is there a need to resort to another world of ideas and values which cannot become present to us, which we do not meet actually in an act of relation. All these means of grasping the world are abstract concepts, not living experience. What is necessary, then, is the complete acceptance of the relational present of all things and persons as they are. However, this cannot be accomplished through fixed precepts, rituals, or an absorption into a transcendent being, all of which have nothing to do with the primal act of meeting. When I distance or separate the world from myself, be it the world of sensation, values, or ideas, I make these things into objects of my understanding, desire, or aspiration. I can use them as I find suitable to my purposes, organize them, evaluate their sundry functions, even convert them into ideas or spiritual entities, but I am not then relating to them in the reality of meeting, where the other is present, standing over against me fully as one being facing another—I am not actually confronting another being.

The more man has lost himself in separation, the greater is the daring required in the acceptance or in the elementary turning away from It and seeing the other as Thou. This does not mean an abandoning of the I, as mysticism presumes, namely, that the I be absorbed or dissolved into the other. The I is as indispensable to the highest relation as to any particular relation, for a relation can take place only between I and a Thou, on any level. Yet it does call for the abandonment of the false self-assertive drive which lets man escape from the unobservable, rather unreliable world of relation into the world of possession and use of things. One must abandon the excessive I-It in which the I asserts itself over the other, trying to possess and use it.

17. *Exclusiveness and Inclusiveness in Relation to God* [126–127]

"Every real relation with a being or a substance (*Wesenheit*) in the world is exclusive. Its Thou is released, steps forth, is singular and substantiated as an opposite. It fills the heavenly spheres." When, however, the Thou becomes an It, its exclusiveness appears as an exclusion of the all. Exclusiveness means here something unique but present in relation; it is an exclusion of objects or what is outside the range of relation. "In the relation with God, unconditioned exclusiveness and unconditioned inclusiveness are one." In this absolute relation, one is not concerned with singular things and existents, earth and heaven, all of which are separations, for everything is included in the relation with the Absolute. To enter into pure relation is not to deny the world but to posit it in its ground, "to see everything in the Thou." One stands in the presence of God not by turning one's back to the world or by gazing at it from a distance, as an observer, but by seeing the world in God. The language of It speaks of the "world here, God over there" or of "God in the world." Complete relation, on the other hand, does not eliminate or leave behind; it comprehends the whole world in the Thou, granting the world its own right and its own truth, "comprehending nothing side by side with God, yet seeing everything in Him" (80). This is not to be taken in a metaphysical sense, for God is not to be identified with the world or man with God. (This will be brought out in Sections 21–23 in connection with the theories of identification and absorption.)

All Buber means to say here is that, when man stands in relation to God, man's being as a whole brings with him all his finite relations with other men and with all things of his lived experience in the world, so that they are with him in his relation to God. Man does not cast them off in order to be in God's presence. On the contrary, man cannot enter into relation with God unless he goes through the relations with fellow-men and the world of things. This is the meaning of the opening statement of Part Three quoted above: "The extended lines of relation intersect in the eternal Thou."

18. *Where Do We Find God?*
   [127–129]

One does not find God by staying in the world or by leaving it. One finds his Thou, which is unsearchable, by going forth toward it with his whole being and bearing toward it everything of the world's being. What one finds is relation, not an object which one may possess or acquire. God is altogether the other but also altogether the same, altogether the present. "He is certainly the *mysterium tremendum* who appears and puts down; but he is also the concealment (*Geheimnis*) of the self-understandable which is nearer to me than my I" (80). By *mysterium* is meant here one that I cannot express in propositions or statements, for he is self-understandable in his closeness to me when I go out to meet him. When I seek the ground of the life of things and conditions, I come upon the insoluble;

The relationship with God ⊅ both I-You and I-It. *

and if I contend against them, I face nothingness. But when I sanctify life I meet the living God. In the first, I seek to understand life in terms of causes of things by other things; and if I cannot find the cause, or I deny it, I have no ground to stand on: I face an insoluble problem or nothingness. In the second, my relation is life as an act of meeting with the living God.

Man may be disappointed by the fact that his relation to a particular Thou must turn into one of I-It. Every particular Thou, when the moment of relation breaks up, becomes an It, an object of experience and use. (See Section 4e, "Passing from Thou to It.") But man's sense of Thou, the inborn Thou, strives *above* all particular ones, not *away from* them, toward the eternal Thou. Each particular relation leads to the Absolute. This striving is not as if one were seeking something. "In truth there is no God-seeking, because there is nothing where one may not find him" (81). It would be foolish for a man to deviate from his life-path to search for God, for he would then surely miss Him. The right life-path *is* the way to God. Rather, going his way, he might wish it were *the* way, and the strength of his wish would express his striving. Each relational event with a particular Thou is a station from which man gets a glimpse into that which brings fulfilment in the relation with the Absolute. Thus, in all the particular relations man does not participate directly in the highest event, yet participates in it insofar as he awaits it. Awaiting this event, that is, going out to meet it, is in itself participation in the relation with the Absolute. "He goes his way awaiting, not searching." This gives him equanimity toward all things. But he does not turn away from them when he has found the one in which he meets everything, for they all participate in the way toward this one. Man will still have to dwell in the things, for "this finding is not an end of the way but only its eternal center. It is a finding without seeking, a discovering of that which is most primal and the prime" (81). What man finds in the Center, that is, in his relation with the Absolute, is the fulfilment of all relations with fellowmen and all things of the world. In this respect, the prime relation stands in the center of all of man's living experiences and is in them in all his encounters.

The primal relation is present from the very start in the sense of Thou, which cannot be satisfied until it has found the infinite Thou. This presentness has to become real through the reality of sanctified life. The inborn Thou of man strives toward the complete relation, which can take place only in the meeting with the Absolute Thou. This is how man sanctifies his life. God is not a derivative of something or a self coming out of the self-contemplating subject. He is not a deduction from something "given" but the immediate, enduring Being over against us, "which properly can only be addressed but not expressed" (82). If we try to express the essence of God, whether as the prime cause of nature, a power of the world, or a self-thinking entity, we make Him into an object of our understanding, an It. But if we address Him, we turn to Him as Being which we encounter in relation.

19. *No Dependence but Partnership* [129–130]

There are those who want to regard the essential element of relation with God as a feeling called dependence, more specifically, a feeling of creatureliness. We may not disregard this element, but to give it unique emphasis is to misconstrue the character of complete realtion, which does not take place *in* the soul but *between* the I and the Thou. No matter how essential feelings may be, they only accompany the fact of relation. Feelings are part of the dynamics of the soul, in psychology, in which they compete with each other in opposite directions. Each feeling has its polar tension. "Every feeling is conditioned by an opposite" and gets its meaning from itself and its opposite, such as love-hate, pleasure-displeasure, dependence-independence. If, then, the absolute relation, which includes all relative relations but is not, like them, particular or partial, is reduced to an isolated, delimited feeling, it becomes a relativized element of psychology. From this point of view, the absolute or complete relation may be conceived only in a bipolar way, as the *coincidentia oppositorum* or the unity of opposite feelings.

In this bi-polar tension between feelings, the religious person may often suppress one of the poles from his reflective consciousness, which can then be brought back to consciousness only through the purest and deepest recollection. He may, for example, suppress a feeling of disbelief in favor of belief, or hate in favor of love, and be aware only of his feeling of belief or love, but not of the opposite feeling until he brings it back through recollection and sees the two as opposites. But in pure relation the two opposites are together, always in a state of mutuality, such as freedom and dependence, neither limiting the other, as in psychology. "Yes, you have plainly felt dependent in pure relation as you are capable of feeling in no other, and plainly also free as never and nowhere before—creaturely and creatively. Here you no longer had the one confined by the other but both unconditioned and both together." As for your sense of dependence, you always know in your heart that you need God, but you may not know that, in the fulness of His eternity, He needs you. "How could there be man if God did not need him? And how could you be? You need God in order to exist, and God needs you—even for that which is the meaning of your life." To speak of "God who becomes" is idle and presumptuous talk, meaning an incomplete God, perhaps an idea in the making. But we know in our heart that there is a becoming of the existing God, the becoming of our entering-in-relation with Him Who is. "The world is not divine sport; it is divine destiny. That there are the world, man, the human person, you and I has divine meaning" (83–84). We must submit to creation, which glows in us, but we also "take part in it, meet the Creator, offer ourselves to Him as helpers and partners" (84).

20. *Prayer and Sacrifice* [130–131]

"Two great servants pass through the ages—prayer and sacrifice." The supplicant pours himself out in dependence and knows how to make an effect on God even though he may not obtain anything from Him. "For when he does not desire anything he sees his effect burning in the highest flame." As for sacrifice, one ought not to despise the servant of old who thought God desired the scent of his burnt offering. He knew that one can and should give something to God. And this everyone knows "who offers to God his small will and meets Him in the grand will." Man speaks nothing

but "Thy will be done," but truth speaks for him further, "through me whom Thou needest." What differentiates prayer and sacrifice from magic is that the latter
seeks to produce an effect without entering-in-relation
but by practicing devices in the void, whereas the former two place themselves before the Presence "in the
completion of the sacred primal word, signifying mutual
effect. They speak Thou and they hear. To want to
understand pure relation as dependence means to want
to deprive one bearer of the relation, and thus relation
itself, of reality" (84). If man is not independent of
the "other" with whom he is to enter-in-relation, whether it be another man or God, relation as such cannot
take place.

II. Duality of Being and Unity

21. *The Self and Oneness* [131–133]

Considered from the opposite side, from that of the
I, the same abolition of relation occurs when the absorption or transformation of the I into the Self is regarded
as the essential element of the religious act. This may
occur by eliminating from the Self everything conditioned by the I, or by conceiving the Self as the One-
Thinking-Being. The first view maintains that God
enters into the being which is emptied of the I, or this
being is absorbed into God. Thus at the highest moment
of the religious act the saying of Thou ceases, as the
duality has been overcome. The second view sees the

Self standing in immediacy to itself as the divine Oneness. Here, too, there is no saying of Thou; in truth there is no duality at all. There is no I as an independent existent in the oneness of God, as distinguished from a Thou. Such oneness is neither I nor Thou. "The first believes in the unification of the human with the divine, the second in their identity" (85). Both views assume an existent beyond I-and-Thou, the one regarding it as being formed through ecstasy, rising to a point where the I merges with the Absolute, the other as a self-revealing existent in itself, such as the self-contemplation of the thinking Subject. "Both abolish relation, the first, as it were, dynamically as the I is swallowed by the Thou, which now, however, is no longer Thou but the Single-Being. The other does it, as it were, statically in that the Self, freed from the I, knows itself as the Single-Being" (85). According to the dependence theory, the I, which is one of the bearers of the world-span of pure relation, is so weak and hollow that its ability to carry its end is no longer trusted. In the first view of absorption, the span disappears at its termination; in the second view, it is treated as a surmountable delusion. In the former, that which stands between I and the Absolute is eliminated in the final act of absorption; in the latter, the I and the between must be recognized as unreal.

These two doctrines of absorption refer to the great statements of identification, the one especially to Jesus' saying, according to John (17:11, 21), "I and the Father are one," and the other to Sandilya's teaching "That all-embracing, this is my Self in the inner heart." These sayings lead in opposite directions, the first issuing from a mythical stature and developing into a doctrine, and the second starting as a doctrine and ending in the life of a person also of mythical stature. Thus, in the first, "the Christ of the Johannine tradition, the word that once became flesh, leads to the Christ of Eckart, whom God begets in eternity in the human soul." In the second, the coronation formula of the Upanishad, which says, "This is the real, it is the Self, and it is you," leads to the Buddhist dethronement formula: "A Self and what belongs to a Self cannot be grasped in truth and reality" (86). Buddhism designates five groups of grasping the world of experience— material shape, feeling, perception, the impulses, and consciousness—all of which are impermanent, suffering, not-Self. This world is empty of Self and of what belongs to Self; hence the Self cannot be grasped in this world in truth.

22. *Unification* [133–134]

John's Gospel is actually one of pure relation, notwithstanding the reference to "I and the Father are one." Father and son or, as we say, God and man, equal in being, are the real "two bearers of the primal relation." Issuing from God to man, it is a mission and command; from man to God, it is looking and hearing. Between both it is called knowledge and love in which the son, "though the Father dwells and works in him, bows to the 'Creator' and prays to Him" (86–87). Modern attempts to interpret this relation in terms of an I to the Self taking place in man are futile, as they are an abrogation of reality.

But, one may ask, shall we doubt the veracity of mysticism which tells of the experience of unity without duality? In answer, Buber says, "I know not of one but two kinds of occurrence in which one has become unaware of duality. Mysticism sometimes confuses them in speech. I, too, did it once." (88).

A. UNIFICATION OF THE SOUL

The experience of unity of the soul occurs *within* man, not in relation between him and God. When this happens, through the ingathering of all of one's powers into the core of his soul, one's being stands alone in exaltation facing a decisive moment, whether to accept this as the goal in itself or only as a potency. When man feels unified in himself, that is, as a whole, he can enter-in-relation with God, who is the hidden one, and thus fulfil himself in redemption. But man may also fail to act out of his unified self and, by not responding, fall back into dispersal of the self. This depends on his decision, which may be concealed in the destiny of being, and that is a decision to respond to the other or to refrain from responding. Such is the unity which man attains within himself as a human being-as-a-whole. But this is not a unity with an other. The mystic who attains self-unification mistakes it as a unification with an other, outside himself.

B. UNITY OF THE ACT OF RELATION

The other occurrence of unity is the relational act itself, in which one imagines that the two subjects who stand in mutual relation have become one, that is, the I and the Thou have merged in the relation. It is as if mankind and God, who erstwhile stood opposite each other, have now become absorbed in the relation and a deified, glorified Oneness has appeared. But when man comes unto himself out of this transfiguration, he finds himself a split being, one part of it surrendered to nonredemption. What good is it for my soul to be able again to break loose from this world and to enter into unity when this world of necessity remains a non-participant in that unity? "Of what avail is all 'enjoyment of God' to a life that is rent asunder" (86)? If that rich heavenly moment has nothing to do with my poor earthly moment, what does it hold for me as long as I still have to live in all earnest on earth?

One can thus understand the Masters who have renounced the ecstasy of union, which is not really a union. It is like people who are so enraptured by the miraculous embrace in the passion of Eros that they lose all sense of I and Thou in a unity which does not and cannot exist. What the ecstasy of the mystics calls unification is the dynamic absorption in relation. This unity does not merge the I and the Thou in a moment of time, but it is the unity of relation, as such, between the two who encounter each other with such force that neither recognizes the rapture of the other. There is here a borderline overflow of the relational act. The vital unity of this act is sensed so vehemently that its members, the I and the Thou between whom it takes place, seem to fade away and are forgotten as being exclusive to each other in the relation. This is one of the phenomena of the brink at which reality grows hazy. By reality is here meant the relation as it takes place between two beings who do not merge into each other, even as they encounter one another in the overwhelming act. But greater than this riddle "is for us the central reality of everyday earthly hour with its sun breaking on a maple twig and the intimation of the eternal Thou" (89). For every relational encounter with nature is the bearer of a relation with the Eternal.

23. *Identity*

A. ALL-BEING AND SELF-BEING [134–136]

In contradistinction to the teaching of unification is the doctrine of absorption, which claims that the all-being and the self-being are one and the same. Therefore the saying of Thou cannot be vouchsafed as an act of final reality. This claim, however, is negated by its own doctrine. According to a certain Upanishad, Indra, the prince of gods, came to Pradashapati, the creative spirit, to learn how to find the Self. After centuries of apprenticeship he received the right information: "When one rests bounded in deep boundless sleep, that is the Self, that is the immortal, the secured, All-being!" When Indra protested that in such condition there is no distinction between I and the beings, no knowledge of one's Self, as it sinks into annihilation, Pradashapati retorted, "That, my Lord, is exactly the situation" (89–90). What this doctrine, then, calls true being has nothing to do with lived reality, which it debases into a world of illusion. Its instruction of absorption in true being leads not into lived reality but into annihilation, where there is no consciousness and no guiding memory. Man emerging from this experience may only profess the "limiting word of Nonreality" but dare not proclaim it as the Oneness.

B. NO ONENESS OF BEING IN LIVED REALITY [136–139]

Contrary to the above doctrine, we want to cultivate the sacred good of our reality for this life and perhaps for none other that may be closer to truth. There is no oneness of being in lived reality, which is an act of power and depth. Inner reality, too, is an act of mutuality of relation with an other, not with oneself. "The strongest and deepest reality is where everything enters into the action, the whole man without reserve and the all-embracing God, the unified I and the boundless Thou" (90). The unified I is that state of the soul when all its forces have been gathered into it, which is man's decisive moment. But it is not, as in absorption, a disregard of the real person. Absorption wants to preserve only the pure, the durable, and to discard everything else. The ingathering of forces, on the other hand, does not regard the drives as too impure, the sensuous as too peripheral, or the moody as too flitting to be less real. Everything must be taken in and overcome. "It does not want the abstracted Self; it wants the whole, undiminished man. It means, and is, reality" (90).

The doctrine of absorption promises a resting place in the Thinking-One, "that whereby this world is thought," in the pure subject. But in lived reality there is no thinking thing without that which is thought; the two are mutually interdependent. A subject abstracted from an object has no reality. A thinking thing, as such, exists only in thought as its limiting idea without an object, as in the concept of death or its equally impenetrable deep sleep, and, finally, as in the statement of the doctrine of absorption, which is like the condition of deep sleep without consciousness and memory. These are the highest peaks of the language of It. One must respect the sublime power of its vision and at the same time recognize that it may only be experienced but not lived, that is, experienced as an object of contemplation or ecstasy but not lived as relation with another being.

Buddha, the fulfilled one and the one who fulfils, does not say whether there is or is not oneness. He refuses to assert whether one who passes all trials of absorption exists after death in the oneness or does not exist in it. This "noble silence" may be explained in two ways: theoretically, because the fulfilment cannot be stated in categories of thought or a proposition; practically, because the disclosure of its state of being does not form a basis of the true life of salvation. Both explanations belong to the same truth: to treat being as an object of a proposition is to draw it into the antithesis of the world of It, of being and not-being as objects of thought, or logical predicates, where there is no life of salvation. In the envisaged mystery, as in lived reality, there is no assertion "it is so" and "it is not so," it is "being" and not "not-being," but there is "so-and-otherwise," the "being-and-not-being," the indissoluble. In lived reality the contradictions are embraced in the relation. "The primal condition of salvation is the undivided confrontation of the undivided mystery" (92). It is certain that Buddha recognized this. He does not teach a viewpoint but a way. He refutes the assertion that there is no action or power, but maintains that one may walk the way. And he dares to make this one assertion: "There is, O Monks, an Unborn, Unbecome, Uncreated, Unformed. If this were not, there would be no goal. If this is there, the way has a goal" (92).

C. BUDDHA'S GOAL [139–141]

Thus far we may follow Buddha, in keeping with our truth of meeting. One step further, however, would be going contrary to the reality of life. For in truth and reality, which are not drawn out of ourselves but are granted to us, we know that if Buddha's goal "is only one of the goals," it cannot be ours; and if it is *the* goal it is falsely designated. Furthermore, if it is one of the goals the way may lead to it, and if it is *the* goal then the way only leads closer to it; that is, Buddha's goal, being what it is, determines his way in trying to reach it or at most come closer to it. Buddha's goal is the "abolition of suffering," that is, of becoming and passing, or "the release from the wheel of births." Its formula for redemption is "henceforth there is no return." Now we do not know whether there is a return of that wheel. We do not go beyond the limits of this life and do not draw the line beyond its own time-limits and laws. But if we knew that there was a return we would not try to escape it, certainly not by yearning for sheer being, but would rather desire that in each state of existence we could speak "the eternal I of the transitory and the eternal Thou of the intransitory" (93).

We do not know whether Buddha leads to the goal of release from the necessity of return, but he does lead to an intermediary goal, which concerns us too, namely, the unification of the soul in itself. However, he leads in the direction not only away from the "thicket of opinion," as is expected, but also away from the "deception of images," which for us it not a deception but rather the trustworthy world of sensibility. Also, his way is "to look away," and when he tells us of becoming innerly aware of what goes on in our bodies he means almost the opposite of the certainty gained by our senses. "And he does not lead the unified being any further to that supreme saying of Thou which is accessible to it. His innermost decision seems to point to the abolition of the ability to say Thou" (94). Buddha himself knows how to say Thou, but he does not teach others, for the simple confrontation of being with being is alien to the kind of love where "everything which has become is contained in the breast without limit." Buddha's relation with his pupils was direct, that is one of love, but he did not teach the doctrine of love. For he taught them to extinguish the flames of life which are the pangs of Becoming eternally burning in their breast. (However, it should be mentioned that one tradition records that Buddha said, of those who have not yet entered the way, "they are sure of heaven if they have love and faith towards me.")

No doubt Buddha also knows, in the depth of his silence, how to say Thou to the primal ground, but he passes over this in silence. Nevertheless, his following among the nations, "the Great Vehicle," has acted contrary to his way. "It has addressed itself to the eternal Thou of man in the name of Buddha. And the coming Buddha that it awaits—the last of the universal age— is the one by whom love is to be fulfilled" (94). Buber's references to Buddha are to the historical person Gautama or Shakyamuni, who lived from 560 to 480 B.C. There are other Buddhas or Enlightened Ones past and future. By the "Coming Buddha" Buber probably means Metteye, who is represented as the personification of Loving-Kindness. There is also the concept that a Buddha is not a man but a spirit, a vehicle of salvation.

24. *Spirit, The Self, and The World* [141–143]

"The whole doctrine of absorption has its ground in the enormous illusion that the human spirit, recoiling upon itself, takes place in man. In truth, it takes place outside of man—between man and that which is not he" (94). The recoiling spirit denies the meaning of relation as a between and draws that which is not-man into man. Hence God and the world, or the others with whom man relates, must be conceived in the soul, and this is the illusion, that it takes spirit to be a soul. In Buber's account of relation, spirit is not a substance or being but that which occurs in the act of relation between two beings. That is, spirit is the relation as such, and not some kind of soul-being. "I proclaim, O friend," says Buddha, "that in this fathom-high ascetic body, afflicted with sensations, there dwells the world and the becoming of the world, and the abolition of the world, and the way that leads to the abolition of the world" (95). This is true, yet in the last analysis it is not true. The world is in me as an appearance, as I am in it as a thing. But neither is actually in the other. We are drawn into each other as a contradiction in thought which is inherent in the world of It. But the contradiction is abolished in the Thou relation, which releases me from the world so that I may communicate with it. The I-Thou relation frees me from seeing the world as a distanced object of causal connections and mediated observations, so that I may enter into immediate relation with all things in the world.

I bear within me the sense of Self which cannot be included in the world. There is the sense of being that the world bears within it, which cannot be included in the appearance. But this is the condition of the world as world (*Welthaftigkeit*) and not some conceivable will. Similarly, the Self is the condition of the I as I (*Ichhaftigkeit*) and not the "knowing subject." These two are further irreducible, and one who disregards their finality thwarts their comprehensible (*begriffbaren*), though not their conceivable (*begrifflichen*), sense. One can understand the Self and the world as concepts which are only abstractions of the person and the world with which one relates in reality. But in relation the particular sense of being, which is peculiar to the Self and the world, respectively, and which cannot be reduced further by concepts, comes into play. The world, as such, and the I, as such, relate not as subject-object, but in their *Welthaftigkeit* and *Ichhaftigkeit*, or as subject-subject.

The origin or abolition of the world is not in me, but neither is it without me. It is, in general, not given but occurs all along, and the occurrence is connected *with* me as well as dependent *on* me—on and with my life, my decision, my deed. However, this does not depend on confirming or denying the world in my soul, but rather on how I let my soul take its attitude toward it, toward life. That is, it depends on how I communicate with the world, whether by distancting or by entering-in-relation, in the one looking at it as an object of experiencing and using, in the other as a subject with whom I communicate in immediacy or as I and Thou.

In real life the soul's attitudes may cross each other in different ways. But he who experiences his attitudes only in his soul is without the world, no matter how full of ideas he may be. All the acts, enthusiasms, and mysteries that may stir within him do not touch the world's shell. He who redeems his own Self alone, without concern for the world, is neither harmful nor beneficial to the world. But he who deals with it faithfully and applies himself to it cannot be godless either. If we love the real, which never wants to be abolished, and dare to embrace it, we shall reach it in the meeting.

"I know nothing of a 'world' and a 'world-life' that might separate man from God. What is thus designated is life with an estranged world of It, which experiences and uses" (96). (See Section 14, "Alienation.") One who in truth goes forth to meet the world also goes forth to meet God. Ingathering and going forth need each other as one. Ingathering all the limited or finite relations is one and the same act as going forth to meet the Infinite. God embraces the all and is not it, as He embraces my Self and is not it. This cannot be expressed adequately, and that is why there are such expressions of acts and such words as I and Thou, encounter, dialogue, spirit, and language, which are the prime acts of spirit—the word in eternity. These are the articulated forms of relation between mutually exclusive beings which meet in an embracing act and yet are not merged into each other, contrary to what the theories of absorption claim.

III. Our Existence in the Presence

25. *Religious Antinomy* [143–144]

"Man's 'religious' situation—his existence in the Presence—is characterized by its essentially insoluble antinomy" (97). This is so by its very nature. One who accepts the thesis and rejects the antithesis violates the sense of the situation; one who tries the synthesis destroys it; one who wants to relativize it does away with it; and one who tries to get around it offends it. The sense of the situation is that, in all its antinomy, it is lived, always again and anew, as something unforeseeable, unpreconceivable, and unprescribable. This may be clarified by comparing it with the philosophical antinomy. Kant has relativized the philosophical conflict between necessity and freedom by assigning the former to the world of appearance and the latter to the world of being. The two positions, having validity in different worlds, are thus no longer contradictory. But necessity and freedom must be meaningful in reality, as I stand before God and not just ideationally. I face the paradox of knowing that I am in one's power and of knowing at the same time that it depends on me. This paradox cannot be overcome by assigning each position to a different world, as Kant does. I must assume responsibility of living them both in one, for when lived they are one.

The nature of man's existence in relation with the Presence of God is to be understood in terms of the occurrence of the relation itself. Something happens when man is confronted with the Absolute in the act of relation. If, however, we try to understand this hap-

pening conceptually, we are faced with antinomies of
finite and infinite, necessity and freedom, relative and
absolute. As concepts all these are irreconcilable. The
main difference which Buber finds between himself and
Kant is that the latter posits a conceptual duality of
being (*noumenon*) and appearance (*phenomenon*)
which cannot be brought together, whereas he himself
deals with a living duality of being and being which
can enter into mutual relation. According to Kant,
man's existence in the Presence of God is that of a
rational mind which has no specific faculty of knowing
God and can at best conceive Him as "merely a relative supposition of a being," as a moral necessity, or
as a relative unifying principle. For Buber, on the other
hand, man's existence in the Presence is that of a being
standing in relation to another being. Man gains this
knowledge through the very act of entering-in-relation.

26. *Latency and Actuality of the Thou* [144–148]

"An animal's eyes have the power of real language."
Without sound and gesture they express the anxiety
of becoming, most powerfully when they repose entirely in their glance. This state of mystery is known
only to the animal, which can open but not reveal i
to us. The language in which it is spoken is anxiety—
a stirring of the creature between the realms of vege-
table-like security and spiritual hazard, the hazard being
that it may venture into the unknown meeting in relation, which entails a risk. "This language is the faltering
voice of nature under the first grip of spirit before i
surrenders to the spirit's cosmic risk which we call man

But no utterance will ever repeat what the faltering knows to convey" (98).

"I look sometimes into the eyes of a cat." The domestic animal did not acquire its gift of the truly speaking glance from us, but gained only the aptitude to direct it toward us monstrous beings. In this glance, as it lights up, there is something of amazement and questioning which was not there in the primal anxiety. This cat, no doubt, started to look at me by asking, "Is it possible that you mean me?" "Do I concern you?" "Do I exist for you?" The *I* means for the cat a designation of selfhood without an ego, which we do not have. This glance further asks, "What is that human glance of yours with its power of relation coming from you and surrounding me?" The animal's glance expresses this anxiety only for a fleeting moment. Man's glance lasts longer but ceases to be a human glance. The animal and man meet in a flash of a relational event and step out of it as quickly. "This," Buber says, "has happened to me several times. In no other occurrence have I known so deeply the transitoriness of reality in all relations with beings, the sublime melancholy of our lot, that every single Thou is destined to become It" (99).

Ordinarily, there is at least a brief day between the morn and the eve of the event, but here, in the meeting with the animal, they rushed fiercely into one another, the Thou appearing and disappearing, leaving us in doubt whether the burden of the world of It was really lifted from the beast and man even for a moment. Was there actually a moment of true relation between man and animal? Man could meditate on it, but the animal could only sink from its faltering glance back into speechless anxiety. Recalling his encounter with the cat, Buber writes again; "How powerful is the continuance of the world of It, and how delicate are the appearances of the Thou! So much can never penetrate the crust of the state of things. O, you lump of catgold! Looking at you once I first understood that *I* is not something 'in me,' yet with you I was only bound up in me. Then the event took place only in me, not between me and you" (100). Nevertheless, when a living being, animal or man, arises from things and proceeds toward me in speech, though very briefly, it is nothing but Thou for me. It is not the relation that gives way but the actuality of immediacy. Even love cannot tarry in the immediate relation; it abides only in the change of actuality and latency. Every Thou in the world is bidden, by its very nature, to become It or to enter repeatedly into the state of things. Only one Thou never ceases to be Thou for us. Latency is here always actuality. He who knows God may know the distance between them, but he never knows the absence of God's Presence. Only, we are not always there to meet the Presence. Whatever one says of God as He or It always is in allegory. "But if we speak Thou to him, then the mortal sense has put the unbroken truth of the world into a word" (101).

27. *Individuation in Relation* [148]

Real relation is exclusive; the other breaks into it to avenge its being excluded. The other wants to be accepted by me directly, immediately. "Only in the relation with God are unconditioned exclusiveness and unconditioned inclusiveness one, in which the all is comprised" (101). Every relation in the world is based on individuation, which makes it possible for different beings to know each other, and also makes it possible to know and be known fully. This is the limitation of every real relation. In complete relation with the Absolute, however, my Thou embraces my Self without being this Self; my limited knowing passes into being known without limit. Again, every real relation takes place in an interchange of actuality with potentiality. Every Thou must become an It in order to become a Thou again. But in pure relation the potential is like actuality's breathing, in which the Thou is always present without changing into an It. "The eternal Thou is *Thou* in its very being; only our kind of being makes it necessary for us to draw this Thou into the world and language of It" (101). The Absolute Thou does not change into an It, but we may speak of Him in terms of the world of It, because of the limitations of our own being.

28. *Primal Duality* [148–149]

"The world of It has sequence in space and time. The world of Thou has no sequence in either. It has its connection in the Center in which the extended lines of the relations intersect—in the eternal Thou" (101). In pure relation the privileges of the world of It are abolished before the great privilege by virtue of which there is a continuum in the world of Thou. (See Section 7c, "Prerogative of the Ordered World.") The world of It is noncontinuous in space and time. In pure relation this separation does not prevail, since the relation is immediate and continuous while it lasts. However, the act of relation lasts only for a brief moment, and when it ceases, its Thou turns into an It. Other relations that follow are not repetitions of the previous ones, for each relational act is unique and never duplicated. In this sense, one relation may be said to be isolated from all others. Yet the isolated moments of relation combine into a connected world-life. These moments are indeed brief and isolated from each other, but their occurrences form a living continuum. By virtue of this great privilege, the world of Thou has a formative power, so that the spirit can penetrate and transform the world of It. We are thus not abandoned to estrangement from the world and to depersonalization of the I. Each moment of relation, which is an act of the spirit, has its effect on the world of It. Each time that man steps out of that moment and the Thou becomes an It the world is not estranged, because it carries with it the erstwhile actual relational occurrence. The I is thus never actually isolated from the Thou, even when the latter is turned into an It, for man may always return to the state of relation. We might say that the Thou is always potentially in the I-It, because man has the potency of again entering into a relationship of I-Thou. This is man's privilege of the return.

To return is to recognize the Center again and to turn toward it. In this act of being, man's power of relation rises again from under the heap, streaming through all the spheres and renewing our world. This may extend to the metacosmos—the world in relation to that which is not-world. In the metacosmos is the primal form of duality, which, in its human form, is the twofold communication in the two primary word-pairs. In the metacosmos there is a foreboding of the double movement, one a turning *away from* the primal ground so that the all is preserved in the becoming, and the other a turning *toward* the primal ground so that the all may be redeemed in being. The mutual relation of the world and not-world is designated by Buber as a metacosmos in its primal form of duality, where the original double movement of turning away or distancing and turning toward or entering-in-relation takes place. Through this double movement a world of things emerges, becomes, as objects of our experience and use, which is the world of It, but without abolishing the all, without splintering the metacosmos itself. For there is also the movement toward the primal ground through the word-pair I-Thou, which redeems the state of distancing, that is, the world of It. The It may thus again be turned into a Thou, but this can take place only through the act of return, which is a free human decision. (See Section 12 on the relational event of return, which is man's destiny as freedom.) In the primal duality, "Both are by destiny unfolded in time; by grace enfolded in timeless creation, which is incomprehensibly at the same time a release and a preservation, a granting of freedom and a binding. Our knowledge about duality is speechless before the paradox of the primal concealment" (102).

IV. Pre-eminence of Relation with Man

29. *The Sphere of Speech* [149–151]

The three spheres of relation are, first, life with nature, which is arrested at the threshold of speech; second, life with man, which assumes speech forms; and third, life with spiritual beings, which is without speech but bears witness to it. In each sphere, in its own manner, we glance at the rim of the eternal one, who binds all the spheres but is not bounded by any of them. The one present radiates through all the spheres, but we can remove each of them from the present, that is, from the moment of relation. We can lift the "physical" world of consistency from life with nature, the "psychical" world of sensibility from life with man, and the "noetic" world of validity from life with spiritual beings. But in their distancing from lived experience these spheres lose their translucent character and can then become objects of use. They are dulled even when we give them such illuminating names as Cosmos, Eros, and Logos. These are mere abstracts from real life with nature, man, and the Absolute, respectively. "In truth, there is a Cosmos for man when the all becomes his home with a holy hearth at which he sacrifices; there is an Eros for him when all beings become images of the eternal and his communion with them becomes revelation" (103). The eternal is not revealed as an image, but man's relation to all beings assumes the images of love, which is the true relation to human beings when man directs himself toward God.

There is Logos only when one addresses the hidden one with work and service in spirit, not through the mediation of a Logos concept but in immediacy, which is spirit. All three—Cosmos, Eros, Logos—have meaning for man only when they articulate his relation to God in all spheres: Cosmos as the place of sacrifice, Eros as communality, and Logos as immediacy in spirit. (See Section 10b on direction and Section 20, "Prayer and Sacrifice.") The portals of the presentness of the word can be an image, man's speech, or a creature's muteness. But in complete meeting with the Divine Absolute these portals merge into one, and man cannot tell which he passes through. Any one of the three spheres will lead man to his relation with the Absolute, and in this relation the spheres intersect and are not distinguishable as to which one brought him into it.

Nevertheless, we may consider the sphere of life with man as pre-eminent, because in this sphere alone language completes itself in speech and counterspeech; the articulated word meets its response in word. Here the primal word goes back and forth in the same form, the address and the encounter in the same tongue, I and Thou standing not only in relation but also in full open speech (*Redlichkeit*). Here the moments of relation are bound together through being immersed in the element of language. That which confronts blossoms forth into full reality of the Thou. Here alone is the undiminished reality of seeing and being seen, knowing and being known, loving and being loved. This is the main portal which encompasses both side portals, leading them into its opening. "Relation with man is virtually comparable to relation with God in that true address is granted true response, only that in God's response everything—the all—reveals itself as speech" (104–105).

30. *Not in Isolation* [151–153]

Why cannot solitude too be a gate? Why must confrontation with the Absolute be only through other beings? Cannot communion with oneself be transformed into communion with the hidden? It would seem that only one who is no longer attached to finite beings is worthy of confronting the Infinite. It depends on the kind of solitude that is meant here. There are two kinds. If the kind that turns away from experiencing and using things as objects or It is meant, it is true of all acts of relation, not only those with the highest Being. But if solitude means absence of relation, as such, with man or the world, then God will accept only those who turn to others and not those who turn away from them. One who lives with those who are present through relation must be bound up with them in real life. Only one who is thus bounded is in readiness for God, for only such a one brings human reality into the presence of God's reality.

There are yet two other kinds of solitude, according to application. If the solitude is for purification of the bounded before he approaches the holiest of holies, then it is what we have all been created for. But if it is a kind of dwelling on a high mound for conversation with oneself, or for the self-gratification of one's soul, then it is a debasement of the spirit into spirituality; self-deluded man fancies that he has God in him and speaks to Him. Spirit, which is relation, turns into spirituality, which is an attempt to gratify oneself not by meeting God, but by taking hold of Him as an object to satisfy one's pleasures. "But truly, though God embraces and dwells in us, we never have him in us. And we speak with him only when speaking is no more within us," but between us and an other (106).

31. *God is no Substitute for Idols* [153–155]

It has been said that man believes either in God or in idols, that is, in some finite good, such as nation, art, power, knowledge, which he can elevate to an absolute state and interpose between himself and God. Then all that is needed to shatter these idols, according to this view, is to prove that they are conditioned and not absolute goods; the wayward religious act will then return of itself to its appropriate object, namely, God. This conception presupposes that man's attitude toward his idolized finite goods is essentially the same as his attitude toward God, differing only as to the respective object of worship. Erring man could then be saved by substituting the true object for the false one. But in truth the two attitudes are not at all the same. Man's relationship toward a "particular something" that supplants eternity always refers to an experienced, usable being, an It, that is an object. The reason why man worships finite goods is that he wants to gain benefits from them as objects he may possess and use at will. It is this relationship toward the impenetrable world of It that blocks the direction toward God. Only the relation of saying Thou can remove the blocking. One who is obsessed by idols, that is, by the will to possess, has no way to God except through a return. This requires not just a change of goal or end-in-view, but also a complete change in movement, that is, turning from the movement of distancing to that of entering-in-relation. We may cure the obsessed man by awakening him toward becoming bounded, but not by directing his obsession toward God. If he remains in his obsession and calls on God, he is just calling on another idol by a different name. This is blasphemy, as when one places an offering on an altar desecrated by an idol after breaking the idol, without replacing the altar itself by one that is consecrated to the true God.

If a man loves his wife in true presentness, he sees in her eyes a ray of the eternal Thou. But he who wants to overpower her with his lust sees the eternal only as a phantom. One who serves his people with self-denying devotion means God. But he whose nation is an idol to whom he would offer everything because it enhances his own image will not see the truth even if we make that image loathsome to him. And a Mammon-slave who is unable to say Thou to God will not say Thou to money either. To him money will always be nothing but an It, his object of use and lust. He cannot serve two masters, but must learn to serve differently. Substituting God for an idol is not real conversion; it just replaces the idol with a phantom called "God." The idol still lingers on in the new worship as a ghost. For God cannot be possessed.

32. *The Single one Cannot Reach God* [155–157]

"Some speak of the 'religious' person as one who need not stand in relation to the world and beings, because the social stage which is determined from without is here surpassed by the power acting only from within" (108). The contention here is that one who wants to reach God is above all social relations, whether family, community, or nation. He can reach God from within his own soul. This is a confusion of two social concepts, one of community, which is structured out of relations, and the other of a collective, that is a massing together of man-units which in modern times has become manifest as the absence of relation. The community is the work of the same forces that operate in the relation between man and God, except that the latter is a confluence of all the finite relations. One who sees fellowman in relation of I-Thou can thus also relate to God as I to a Thou. But if man sees fellowmen as units of a collective, held together by an outside force without inner primal relation, he tends to regard them as objects of use only. Such a man is godless, for "one cannot apportion one's life between a real relation to God and an unreal I-It connection with the world, truly pray to God, and make use of the world." If one knows only how to use the world, one tends to know God also only in terms of using Him. One's prayer then falls on nothingness. "He who addresses himself to the nameless out of the night, yearning through his chamber's window, is the atheist, not the godless one" (108–109). An atheist may indeed yearn for God but is troubled by the fact that he cannot find Him and hence denies any knowledge of Him or His existence. But the godless one is not concerned with God at all and does not seek any relation to Him.

It is further maintained that the religious man steps as a single one before God, detached from fellowman and the world, because he has surpasssed the stage of a moral being. The latter is still burdened with duty and guilt, with responsibility for deeds, because he is conditioned by the tension between what is and what ought to be and may thus still devote his heart to bridging the gap. But the religious person, it is claimed, has risen above this. As he steps before God, he is commanded to cast off responsibility and self-demand. Here he has no will of his own; every ought is dissolved into conditioned being. The world may still exist but is no longer valid for him. He has to perform what is demanded but without obligation to this world, which is nothing but illusion. His obligations are only to God.

This is an untenable view, as it assumes that God created the world and man for mere appearance. To be sure, he who meets God is above duty and guilt; this is not because he has escaped the world, however, but rather because he has come closer to it. "One bears duty and guilt only towards the stranger; towards the intimate person one is well disposed and full of love" (110). He who steps before the Face in the full presentness sees the world fully present and can say Thou to the Being of all beings. Then there is no tension between the world and God. Man then does not divest himself of responsibility. He exchanges the finite for the infinite, the sway of loving responsibility for the universal inclusiveness in the Face of God. He has given up the moral judgment of condemning evil-doers, for he looks at the "evil one" only as being in greater need of love, as demanding his deeper responsibility. Nevertheless he still has to practice decision until death, the calm coming-to-a-decision for the right deed. Man who stands in the Face of God relates to fellowman as part of creation, which is in need of love and responsibility. By assuming this responsibility towards fellowman one becomes a partner in God's creation and redemption. Thus man can reach God through communality and not as a single one, detached from all other men and from the world of things. "Here the doing is not for naught; it is intended, commissioned, needed—it belongs to creation. But this doing is no longer imposed on the world; it grows on it as if it were not-doing" (110).

V. The Eternal

33. *In Human Life* [157–160]

The eternal as the primal phenomenon, which is present here and now and which we call revelation, is manifest in the fact that man emerges out of the meeting not the same as he entered into it. That moment is not an experience stirring *in* the soul. It happens with man, between him and the eternal. Coming out of this event, man has something more grown upon him of which he knew not before the event and whose origin he cannot properly designate. The scientific world-orientation may arrange the source of the new elements according to unbroken causality; but for us, who are concerned with real viewing of reality, the subconscious or any other soul-apparatus is of no avail. Reality is what we receive in such a manner that we know it is given to us and that we did not have it before we received it. This is not a "content" but a presentness of a power that includes three undifferentiated moments, which may nevertheless be viewed separately.

First is the fulness of real presentness, connectedness, and inclusiveness without knowing how it is constituted and without making life easier but rather making it meaningfully much harder. *Second* is the ineffable confirmation, even assurance, of meaning. Nothing can now be meaningless, and the question as to the meaning of life does not exist; moreover, if it did, it would not call for an answer. The meaning cannot be demonstrated or defined; there is no formula for it, yet it is more certain than our own sense-experiences. *Third*, this meaning is not of a life beyond but of this our life, not of another world but of this our world, and it is "in this life and in this world that it wants to be confirmed by us" (112).

The meaning may be received and acted out but not experienced, and that is what it expects of us. (By experience is meant here objectified experience of things, not lived experience, which is the act of relation itself.) The assurance is not locked up within us but wants to be generated through us into the world. It is generated in the meeting with the Absolute, as in a partnership. This meaning cannot be translated into universal, accepted knowledge, and by the same token its confirmation cannot be prescribed or recorded as valid tradition of an ought—either in a logical, conceptual system or in ethical norms handed down by tradition. Each act of relation is confirmed in and of itself. One confirms meaning with his own being, in his own life. No precept leads us toward meeting, and none leads us out of it. There is no prescribed formula or fixed manner of entering-in-relation or of stepping out of it. What one needs is the acceptance of presentness in order to come into relation, as well as to come out of it after the relation has ceased. One meets with the word Thou on his lips, and one is released from the meeting into the world also with Thou on his lips. When the moment of relation ceases and we enter the world of It, the Thou does not disappear but accompanies us into this world. The mystery from which, wherein, and into which we live remains the same as it was. In its presentness it has become manifest as redemption; we have recognized it but have no knowledge of it whereby to diminish or alleviate its mysteriousness.

"We have come close to God but not any nearer to solving the riddle or removing the veil of Being." We have had a presentiment of redemption but no solution. We cannot tell others that what we have received is the thing to know and do. "We can only go and confirm, and even this not as we 'ought' but as we can—we must." This is the eternal revelation now and here. There is none which might have been different in its prime appearance. God has not named or defined Himself before man in an original, one-time revelation which was different from all subsequent revelations. The word of revelation is, "I am here as the one who is here." The revealing is the revealing. The Being is here, nothing further being said. "The eternal source of power streams, the eternal touch awaits, the eternal voice rings, nothing further" (113). (When Moses asked God for His name, at the revelation of the Burning Bush, the answer was "I am here as I am.") Revelation is thus in the meeting of the two parts of the way. Man, as partner in this act, can prepare only his part of the way and nothing further. The other part comes from God by grace. Revelation occurs when man responds with responsibility for his fellow-creatures to the touch of grace that calls and awaits him. But he cannot go beyond the now and here, beyond the presentness of the act of relation itself. (See Section 16, "Two Parts of the Way.")

34. *The Eternal Thou* [160-161]

The eternal Thou cannot be turned into an It, for it is not measurable even in boundless terms. It cannot be grasped as a sum of attributes, finite or infinite, and it cannot be found or experienced as an object in or outside the world. Even to say, "I believe that he is," is speaking of a He, which is just another word for It, not Thou.

35. *Representation of Revelation* [161]

We turn the eternal Thou repeatedly into an It, a thing according to our being, though not wilfully. The course of God-thing in religion, as it passed through its lights and shadows going away from God and back to Him, the transformation of presentness, image-forming, objectification, conceptualization, dissolution, and renewal are all one way—*the* way. How do presentness and power received in revelation (and, strictly speaking, there are religions only of revelation) become "content" in formulated knowledge, and precepts of doing in theology and ethics? We may distinguish an outer, psychic layer when we consider man, as such, outside history, and an inner, factual layer when we consider the prime phenomenon of religion historically. The two, however, go together.

A. PSYCHIC FACTOR [161-163]

Man desires to have God in continuity of time and space. He is not satisfied with the ineffable manifestation of meaning, because he wants to see it extended into something he can deal with in a gapless spatio-temporal continuum, in which his life may be secured at each point and each moment. Man, who desires this continuity, is not content with the life-rhythm of pure relation, the changes of actuality and latency in which only presentness but not the primal present is diminished. (The primal present is always actuality.) He desires temporal extension, duration. "Thus, God becomes the object of belief. Originally belief complements the acts of relation in time; gradually it replaces them" (115). The constantly renewed movement of being, the ingathering and going forth, is replaced by the repose of an It one believes in, one in which the movement is arrested in a given place and time. The unassured trust that is known to one who struggles as he comes near or is far from God is transformed into the security of the man who seeks to derive profit, the man to whom nothing can happen because he believes in the existence of One who will let nothing happen to him.

Man's thirst for continuity is also not quenched by the living structure of pure relation, in which all moments are one continuum, in the loneliness of the I before the Thou in which man, even after drawing the world in, can still go forth only by himself as a person to meet God. That is, even after man has gathered in all his finite relations with the world and fellowmen, when he goes out to the meeting with the Absolute he must go forth by himself and he alone must take the risk of the meeting. Because of this loneliness, "He desires spatial extension and representation in which the community of believers unites with God. That is how God becomes the object of a cult" (115). By adopting living prayer the cult can be a complement of relation; it says Thou in sensate form. But when personal prayer is no longer carried by the communal prayer, but is separated and replaced by it, communal cult becomes a substitute for the act of relation. It is turned into regulated piety toward something which by its nature cannot be regulated.

In truth, however, pure relation can be established as spatiotemporal stability only when it incorporates the material of life. It cannot be protected; it can only be confirmed, enacted into life. Man can fulfil his relation to God when, within the limits of his power, each day he renews the reality of God in the world. The genuine guarantee of continuity lies in the elevation of the being of the entire community to the status of Thou. Thus temporal human life has the fulness of reality and is activated by relation even when it is in the world of I-It. This gives it genuine stability. "The moments of the highest meeting are here not like lightning in darkness but like the rising moon in a starry night" (116). Similarly, the genuine assurance of spatial continuity lies in the relation of all men in the community with their true Thou, the eternal Thou. These relations of all the I-points to the Center are like the radii of a circle of which the periphery is the community. But what counts is not the community as such, as a static structure, but *communality*, which is acted out in all the radii to the Center. It is this active communality alone which guarantees the genuine duration of the community. As long as time is bounded in relational life as moments of relation, and space is bounded in the community as points of radiating communality, the world stuff of universal duration endures as a human cosmos, embraced in the spirit, which is itself relation. Communality thus appears as the active force arising out of the act of repeated relation with the Absolute, into which each person seeks to enter as and when he gathers within himself all his finite relations with fellowmen. This force cements all persons into a living community, one in which there is mutual responsibility *for* each other as well as respsonsibility *to* God, the Absolute Thou.

B. HISTORICAL FACTOR [163–167]

Meeting with God is a matter not of man being preoccupied with God or a God-idea of another-worldly object, but of confirming meaning in the world. All revelation is a call and a mission. Man repeatedly recoils from it inwardly so that he no longer confronts a Thou. He then conceives God as an object of his inwardly thinking subject, a God-It, and seeks to find Him as a thing. The man who seeks his "I" through self-reflection instead of in living relation with an other cannot find it, because he misses the truth of the relational occurrence in which the I gains its real meaning as a partner in the word-pair I-Thou. Similarly, the man who seek God by reflecting on the given instead of letting the gift take effect in the relation misses both the giver and the gift.

God is always present before him who goes forth on his mission, and the more strongly one fulfils the mission the stronger and more constant is he near God. To be sure, one cannot occupy oneself with God, but one can hold discourse with Him. But he who recoils inwardly on his I makes God into an object, and though he may apparently move toward the prime ground, in truth he turns away from it. Contrarily, he who fulfils his mission, though apparently turning away from it, in truth goes on the way of direction toward God. Direction may be going back and forth and still be a relation with God. (See Section 10b on direction.)

The history of man's relation to God manifests the metacosmic movements of the world, extending to particulars and connecting them, reconciling their coming together and falling apart. This is expressed in the acts of relation, distancing, and return to relation. "In the return the word is born on earth, in the extension it changes into a religious chrysalis, in renewed return it is reborn with new wings" (118). Return means complete, wholehearted turning toward the Thou. When man strays from the way of direction toward God, he has to renew his turning toward Him. There is no wilfulness here, even though the It-movement may sometimes threaten to block the going-out to the Thou.

The mighty revelations which are referred to by the religions and which occurred at great turning points of time, are virtually the same as the quiet ones in all places and times; they are all nothing but the eternal revelation. Revelation is not an occurrence once for all times, or a one-time occurrence of the past only, but takes place at all moments of genuine turning. It does not pour itself through its recipient as through a funnel into the world. It comes upon him, seizes his entire being in all its particularity, and fuses with it. Nor is man just the mouthpiece, like a speaking tube, a tool, but rather an organ sounding according to its own laws. Moreover, sounding means modifying. As a partner in revelation man plays an active role in its modifications each time he enters-in-relation, which is always a new, never repeated act.

There is, however, a qualitative difference in historical times. There is a ripening of time when the suppressed element of the human spirit is ready to break out at the mere touch of the One who touches. The ensuing revelation then grasps it and recasts it into a form of God in the world. Thus, in the path of history, ever new regions of the world and of the spirit, which are transformed into the human element, are summoned to become divine forms; ever new spheres become places for theophany. Not man's peculiar power works here, not the passing through of God, but rather a blending of the human and the divine. The man who is sent forth in revelation takes along an image of God in the eyes of his spirit, not metaphorically but in reality. The spirit too responds through formative looking. "Even though we earthly beings never look at God without the world but only look at the world in God, yet as we look we form eternally God's countenance (*Gottes Gestalt*)" (119).

The countenance, too, is a mixture of Thou and It, congealing into an object of belief and cult but also becoming presentness again through the essence of relation which lives in it. "God is near his countenances if man does not distance them from him," that is, if man does not convert them into objects. Cult and belief unite in a living relation in true prayer whose presence in religions bears witness to their true life, but whose degeneration signifies their degeneration as well. Then the power of relation becomes overlaid with objectification, and man is no longer able to say Thou with his whole being. He may overcome this condition only by stepping out of his false hiding and meeting the infinite, or by emerging from the sheltered temple-dome of regulated cult and prayer into loneliness, where he is sheltered only by the firmament.

To say that this is subjectivism is a gross misunderstanding of its motive. "Life in the Face is life in the One Reality, the only true *objectivum*." The man who goes out to the meeting with the Face wants to save himself from the illusory *objectivum* in the truly existing one, before its truth has been upset by the former. "Subjectivism is making God into a soul, objectivism is making Him into an object, the one being false immutability, the other false liberation, both going astray from the path of reality, both attempting to substitute for it" (120). If God is not near His countenances, it is man who distances them from Him. Man holds down the returning movement and thus effaces the countenances. Then man's cosmos, which is built around the altar, falls apart, and man does not even know what has taken place here.

36. *The Living Word* [168]

What has taken place in the occurrence just described is the decomposition of the word. "The word has its being in the revelation, its effect in the life of the countenance, and it asserts itself in the sway of the departed countenance. Such is the course and countercourse of the eternal and the eternally present word in history." The word appears in its being when the connectedness of I and the world is renewed. It has its effect when there is mutual communication between I and the world, and it asserts itself also when estrangement between I and the world has run its course and has reached its peak. Then there arrives "the great shudder, the holding of breath in darkness and the silence of preparation" of man's part of the way to God.

The way to God is not a circular one. Each new eon makes the return more difficult. God's revelation approaches the sphere which lies between the beings, between us, in our midst. History moves in spirals, each leading into deeper ruination, but also into more profound return. "However, the occurrence which on the part of the world is called return, is on the part of God called redemption" (121).

The partnership between man and God, which the historical spiral indicates, is acted out in the spheres of creation, revelation, and redemption, which Buber calls "the threefold chord in the triad of time." *Creation*, as the divine act of building a cosmos, summons man to participate in creating order out of chaos, to complete the cosmos which God called into being. *Revelation* is the entering-in-relation, when man goes forth with his being-as-a-whole to meet God. *Redemption* is the renewed return after man has gone astray from his path toward God. Through his return, the man who has gathered-in all things in the world and has turned again to God participates in his own and the world's redemption.

PUBLICATIONS OF MARTIN BUBER'S
I and Thou

IN GERMAN

Ich und Du, Martin Buber. First edition. Leipzig: Insel-Verlag, 1923.

Ich und Du, Martin Buber. Berlin: Schocken, 1936.

In *Dialogisches Leben*, Martin Buber. Zürich: G. Müller, 1947.

In *Die Schriften über das dialogische Prinzip*, Martin Buber. Heidelberg: Lambert Schneider, 1954 and 1962.

In *Werke*, Martin Buber. Erster Band. Heidelberg: Lambert Schneider, 1962.

Ich und Du, Martin Buber. Köln: Jakob Hegner, 1966.

ENGLISH TRANSLATIONS

I and Thou, Martin Buber. Trans. Ronald Gregor Smith. Edinburgh: T & T Clark, 1937. Second Edition, with a Postscript by the author added. New York: Charles Scribner's Sons, 1958.

I and Thou, Martin Buber. A new translation, with a Prologue "I and You" and notes by Walter Kaufmann. New York: Charles Scribner's Sons, 1970.

*Corresponding Page References in Walter Kauf-
mann's Translation (1970) and in the Second Edition
of Ronald Gregor Smith's Translation (1958)*

Section in this Book	Kaufmann	Smith	Section in this Book	Kaufmann	Smith
1	53–54	3–4	13a	111–115	61–65
2	54–56	4–6	b	115–117	65–67
3a	56–59	7–8	c	117–119	67–69
b	59–60	8–9	14a	119–120	69–70
c	60–62	9–11	b	120–122	70–72
4a	62–63	11–12	15	123–124	75–76
b	63–65	12–14	16	124–126	76–78
c	65–67	14–15	17	126–127	78–79
d	67–68	15–16	18	127–129	79–81
e	68–69	16–18	19	129–130	81–82
5a1	69–73	18–21	20	130–131	82–83
a2	73–75	21–22	21	131–133	83–85
a3	75–76	22–24	22	133–134	85–87
b1	76–78	24–27	23a	134–136	87–89
b2	78–79	27–28	b	136–139	89–91
6a	80	28–29	c	139–141	91–93
b	80–81	29–30	24	141–143	93–95
c	81–82	30–31	25	143–144	95–96
7a, b	82–85	31–34	26	144–148	96–99
c	84–85	33–34	27	148	99–100
8a	87–89	37–39	28	148–149	100–101
b	89–90	39–40	29	149–151	101–103
c	90–92	40–43	30	151–153	103–104
9	92–95	43–46	31	153–155	104–106
10a	95–96	46–48	32	155–157	106–109
b	96–100	48–51	33	157–160	109–112
11a	100–101	51–52	34	160–161	112
b	101–103	52–56	35	161	112–113
12	103–105	54–56	a	161–163	113–115
a	105–107	56–58	b	163–167	115–119
b	107–111	58–61	36	168	119–120

SELECTED
BIBLIOGRAPHY

Buber's collected writings in the original German are compiled in the following volumes:

Martin Buber, *Werke*. 3 volumes. Heidelberg: Verlag Lambert Schneider. Erster Band: *Schriften zur Philosophie*, 1962. Zweiter Band: *Schriften zur Bibel*, 1964. Dritter Band: *Schriften zum Chassidismus*, 1963.

————— *Der Jude und sein Judentum*. Köln: Joseph Melzer Verlag, 1963.

————— *Hinweise: Gesammelte Essays*. Zürich: Manesse Verlag, 1953.

————— *Nachlese*. Heidelberg: Verlag Lambert Schneider, 1966.

————— *Briefwechsel aus sieben Jahrzehnten*. In 3 Bänden. Herausgegeben und eingeleitet von Grete Schaeder in Beratung mit Ernst Simon und unter Mitwirkung von Rafael Buber, Margot Cohn und Gabriel Stern. Heidelberg: Verlag Lambert Schneider. *Band I: 1897–1918*, 1972. *Band II: 1918–1938*, 1973. *Band III: 1938–1965* (forthcoming).

A full bibliography of Buber's works is given in the following publications:

A Bibliography of Martin Buber's Works 1897–1957. Compiled by Moshe Katanne. Jerusalem: Bialik Institute, 1958. Annotated in Hebrew.

"Bibliography," compiled by Maurice Friedman, in *The Philosophy of Martin Buber*, ed. Paul Arthur Schilpp and Maurice Friedman. La Salle, Illinois: Open Court, 1967. Also contains "Buber's Autobiography."

ENGLISH TRANSLATIONS

A Believing Humanism: My Testament 1902–1965. Trans. and with an Introduction and Explanatory Comments by Maurice Friedman. New York: Simon and Schuster, 1966. A volume of *Credo Perspectives*, planned and edited by Ruth Nanda Anshen.

Between Man and Man. With an Afterword by the author on "The History of the Dialogical Principle." Trans. Ronald Gregor Smith, Afterword trans. Maurice Friedman. New York: Macmillan Paperbacks, 1965.

Daniel: Dialogues on Realization. Ed. and trans. with an Introductory Essay by Maurice Friedman. New York: Holt, Rinehart & Winston, 1964.

Eclipse of God: Studies in the Relation Between Religion and Philosophy. New York: Harper Torchbooks, 1957.

For the Sake of Heaven. Trans. Ludwig Lewisohn. Philadelphia: Jewish Publication Society of America, 1946.

Good and Evil. New York: Charles Scribner's Sons, 1952.

Hasidism and Modern Man. Ed. and trans. Maurice Friedman. New York: Harper Torchbooks, 1966.

I and Thou. Trans. Ronald Gregor Smith. Edinburgh: T & T Clark, 1937. Second edition, with a Postscript by the Author added. New York: Charles Scribner's Sons, 1958.

I and Thou. A new translation, with a Prologue "I and You" and notes by Walter Kaufmann. New York: Charles Scribner's Sons, 1970.

Israel and Palestine: The History of an Idea. Trans. Stanley Godman. New York: Farrar, Strauss and Young, 1952.

Israel and the World: Essays in a Time of Crisis.

Trans. Greta Hort, O. Marx, and I. M. Lask. New York: Schocken Books, 1948.

Moses: The Revelation and the Covenant. New York: Harper Torchbooks, 1958.

On Judaism. Ed. Nahum Glatzer. "The Early Addresses," trans. Eva Jospe, "The Later Addresses," trans. I. M. Lask et al. New York: Schocken Books, 1967.

Paths in Utopia. Trans. R. F. C. Hull. Boston: Beacon Press, 1960.

Pointing the Way. Ed. and trans. and with an Introduction by Maurice S. Friedman. New York: Harper Torchbooks, 1963.

Tales of the Hasidim. Vol. 1: *Early Masters.* Vol. 2: *Later Masters.* Trans. Olga Marx. New York: Schocken Paperbacks, second printing, 1964.

Ten Rungs: Hasidic Sayings. Collected and edited by Martin Buber. Trans. Olga Marx. New York: Schocken Books, 1962 (second printing, 1964).

The Kingship of God. Third, newly enlarged edition. Trans. Richard Scheimann. New York: Harper & Row, 1957.

The Knowledge of Man. Ed. and with an Introduction by Maurice Friedman. Trans. Maurice Friedman and Ronald Gregor Smith. New York: Harper Torchbooks, 1965.

The Origin and Meaning of Hasidism. Ed. and trans. Maurice Friedman. New York: Harper Torchbooks, 1966.

The Prophetic Faith. Trans. from the Hebrew by Carlyle Witton-Davies. New York: Harper Torchbooks, 1960.

Two Types of Faith. Trans. Norman P. Goldhawk. New York: Harper Torchbooks, 1961.

WRITINGS ON BUBER IN ENGLISH

Books

Agus, Jacob B. *Modern Philosophies of Judaism*, Ch. iv. New York: Behrman's Jewish Book House, 1941.

Diamond, Malcolm L. *Martin Buber: Jewish Existentialist*. New York: Harper Torchbooks, 1960.

Friedman, Maurice S. *Martin Buber: The Life of Dialogue*. Chicago: University of Chicago Press, 1955. Paperback edition, Harper Torchbooks, 1960.

————— *Martin Buber: Encounter on the Narrow Ridge*. New York: McGraw Hill, 1968.

The Philosophy of Martin Buber. Eds. Paul Arthur Schilpp and Maurice Friedman. The Library of Living Philosophers, vol. xii. La Salle, Illinois: Open Court, 1967. Descriptive and critical essays by thirty authors and Buber's "Reply to His Critics." Index and Bibliography.

Articles and Reviews

Downing, Christian R. "Guilt and Responsibility in the Thought of Martin Buber," *Judaism*, Winter 1969, pp. 53–63.

Eckardt, A. Roy. "Good and Evil, by Martin Buber," a Review, *The Journal of Bible and Religion*, xxii.1 (Jan. 1954), pp. 46 ff.

Friedman, Maurice S. "Israel and the World, by Martin Buber," a Review, *The Journal of Religion*, xxix.2 (Apr. 1949), pp. 158 ff.

————— "Martin Buber and Christian Thought," *The Review of Religion*, xviii.1–2 (Nov. 1953), pp. 31–43.

————— "Martin Buber's View of Evil," *Judaism*, Vol. 2, No. 3 (July 1953), pp. 239–246.

——————— "Martin Buber's Theory of Knowledge," *Review of Metaphysics*, Dec. 1954.

——————— "Symbol, Myth, and History in the Thought of Martin Buber," *The Journal of Religion*, xxiv.1 (Jan. 1954), pp. 1–11.

Hartland-Swann, J. "Paths in Utopia," a Review, *Philosophy*, xxv, No. 95 (1950), pp. 366 ff.

Kohanski, Alexander S., "Martin Buber's Restructuring of Society into a State of Anocracy," *Jewish Social Studies*, xxxiv.1 (Jan. 1972), pp. 42–57.

——————— "Martin Buber's Philosophy of Judaism," *Judaism*, 24.1 (Winter 1975), pp. 69–81.

Kuhn, Herbert. "Between Man and Man," a Review, *Journal of Philosophy*, xlvi (1949), pp. 75–79.

McCarthy, C. R. "Personal Freedom and Community Responsibility," *Catholic World*, Vol. 203 (June 1966), pp. 165–168.

Morgan, George W., "Martin Buber and Some of His Critics," a Review-Essay, *Judaism*, Vol. 18, No. 2 (Spring 1969), pp. 232–241.

Pfuetze, Paul E. "Martin Buber and Jewish Mysticism," *Religion in Life*, xvi (1947), pp. 553–567.

Potok, C. "Martin Buber and the Jews: His Interpretation of the Path to Hasidism," *Commentary*, Vols. 41 and 42, March and Sept. 1966.

Shaffer, C. R. "Jewish Way of Redemption," *Commonweal*, Vol. 90 (Sept. 19, 1969), pp. 512–515, 574–575.

Tillich, Paul. "Jewish Influences on Contemporary Christian Theology," *Cross Currents*, ii.3 (Spring 1952), pp. 38–42.

——————— "Martin Buber and Christian Thought," *Commentary*, Vol. 6 (June 1948), pp. 515–521.

Woodhouse, Helen. "Martin Buber's 'I and Thou,'" *Philosophy*, xx (1945), pp. 17–30.

A GLOSSARY OF MARTIN BUBER'S TERMS

Selected references to Buber's works in English translation are given by their initials, as follows, and appropriate page numbers:

BH   *A Believing Humanism*
BMM   *Between Man and Man*
EG   *Eclipse of God*
GE   *Good and Evil*
I&T   *I and Thou*
I&W   *Israel and the World*
KM   *The Knowledge of Man*
PW   *Pointing the Way*

Although Buber's terminology does not lend itself to strict definition, his use of concepts and terms is precise and consistent throughout his writings. He says of his own method, "I have learned in the course of my life to appreciate terms. . . . When I find something that is essentially different from another thing, I want a new term. I want a new concept" (KM 197). In the following glossary I do not define but only describe certain terms as Buber has used them in various contexts of his philosophical works, which, taken together, constitute a self-consistent thought-complex. The terms are given in my English translation, with their German equivalent in parentheses.

Absolute. "A power which cannot be identified with any attribute accessible to human understanding. . . ." It cannot be expressed in a proposition or pointed out as "absolute in itself"; it can only be demonstrated in living experience, that is, in meeting. Insofar as we may speak of it at all, "the true absolute can be pointed out as God" (I&W 209).

Absolute Thou (*das absolute Du, das ewige Du*). The

Thou which cannot by its very Being become an It is called the Absolute Thou. It cannot become an object of experience or use. Buber's meaning of the Absolute is in the nature of negative attributes, although he does not teach this doctrine. Positively he expresses it in the attribute of "person" or, rather, "absolute person," but only insofar as it is in relation to another person, which in a sense makes it relative. But that is the paradox of the absolute when spoken of, rather than spoken to.

Alienation (*Verfremdung*). Alienation occurs between the I and the world when man cannot coordinate the two as conceptual entities into one all-embracing totality. He tries to overcome his alienation either by explaining the *I* in terms of natural elements of the world, or the *world* in terms of psychological elements of the I. But when he looks at the two together, he loses his orientation in reality, for neither is a satisfactory explanation of both at the same time. Alienation thus means disorientation, which frightens man by its self-contradiction.

A Priori. Before there is relation with an actual other, there is a state of striving for relation, "the drive that makes everything a Thou," "the *a priori* of relation." This is manifest at the most inchoate level in the life of the child. *See* Inborn Thou.

Art (*Kunst*). The potency of art realizes itself in forming an image of the relation between man and an other. It is not the image taken from the mind of the artist (the I) or from the other he portrays (the Thou), but of that which occurs in the encounter. Art is the image of the between. "To be sure, it is neither the mystery of the things nor that of the spirit which is represented in art, but the relation between the two" (KM 165).

Being (*Wesen, Sein*). This is not a concept from which other concepts may be derived, but the living real-as-a-whole which relates to another real living being-as-a-whole. Being has meaning only insofar as it relates or communicates with another being. A single, solitary being, "the single one," is meaningless.

Being There (*Dasein, da sein*). Relation takes place between one and an other when the one responds, "is there," at the moment he meets the other. The other, however, may not even be aware of this response. What is important is that he is not an object of use by the first, but is accepted as the independent subject in himself that he is (BMM 166).

Between (*Zwischen*). Through the act of entering-in-relation there occurs a "between" man and an other. The between is thus not something that is but always becomes, which is the dynamic of relation. When Buber speaks of "the crisis of the between," he means that the crisis is neither of the soul of individual men nor of the world which determines them, but "of what is between man and man" or man and the world (KM 77; BMM 203).

Category, Category of Being (*Kategorie, Kategorie des Seins*). Buber uses the term category in the original Greek sense of *kategorein*; to say, to speak, to state. Category means that which may be said of a thing. When Buber considers the category of man (*die Kategorie des Menschen*) as a being who relates and distances, he means that this is the most primal thing that may be said of man, not as a species in the chain of animal evolution, but as the kind of being who acts in a certain way which distinguishes him from all other beings.

Cause and Effect, Causality (*Ursache und Folge, Ur-*

sächlichkeit). As concepts of physical science, cause and effect are interdependent coordinates, the occurrence of effect depending on a cause and the force of cause of necessity exercising itself unto an effect. In the relational occurrence there is no such interdependence. Although the Thou is affected by the I, it also affects it, but neither is the cause or effect of the other. There is mutuality of relation between them without mutual dependence. Causality, then, as a concept of producing a change in the other in time is absent from the realm of relation (I&T 30; PW 125).

Cognition, Knowledge (*Erkenntnis, Kennen*). Cognition is one of the four potencies of the act of communication. It may be immediate knowledge of the other, which occurs in the I-Thou relation, or mediated perceptual and conceptual knowledge of objects, as in the I-It connection. In the first, man seeks complete relation with the other in order to recognize his reality. In the second, he is satisfied with experiencing and using the other (KM 163–164).

Collective, Collectivism (*Kollektiv, Kollektivismus*). A collective, as distinguished from a community, is an aggregate of individuals held together by external ties for the purpose of attaining some common goal; examples are a trade union, a political party, a business association. When the particular goal is attained or considered to be unattainable, the collective may dissolve itself. The individual is a subordinate part of the collective, to which he relinquishes all responsibility. Collectivism thus deprives man of his full responsibility and undermines his category *humanum*. It "devours his selfhood" (BMM 80, 110; PW 146, 225).

Communication (*Kommunion, kommunizieren*). Buber

speaks of "communion" and "communicating" as primary acts of relation. Relation, as such, is one of the twofold ways of communication between one being and an other. The opening statement in *I and Thou* may thus be rendered into English as, "To man the world is twofold, according to his twofold communication (*Haltung*)," that is, his actual "bearing" toward an other, rather than "his twofold attitude." The term attitude has a psychological connotation, which is contrary to Buber's intent. Buber would say that man *has* an attitude toward an other, but lives *in* communication with the other (BMM 192; I&T 3).

Community, Communality (*Gemeinschaft, Gemeinschaftlichkeit*). Community is a union (*Verbundenheit*) of persons, each one of whom is an other and all of whom are united in their personal acts of mutual relation, in which they recognize and accept each other as others. In this respect, "Community is an overcoming of *otherness* in living unity." The forming power of community is what may be termed "communality," and that is the relation of each person with the Absolute. Man exists as a person only insofar as he, together with others, forms a community through each one's relation with the Absolute, which is also manifest in interhuman relations. This relation to the Absolute is termed the Center, where communality takes place; community is where theophany takes place. Community or communality has no meaning apart from this Center (I&T 45; BH 151–152; BMM 30–33).

Confirming (*Bestätigung, Bewährung*). In the act of relation one confirms the other, that is, accepts him as he is, without trying to dominate, change, or use him as a means to an end. "Confirming means first of all accepting the whole potentiality of the other. . . ." (KM 71, 79, 182).

Confirming the Meaning of Life. *See* MEANING OF LIFE.

Conversation (*Gespräch*). Conversation between two beings in truth is an act of relation, a dialogue, even when nothing is said in words.

Cosmos (*Kosmos*). As a concept, cosmos is an abstraction from man's life with nature, which is constructed as a physical universe. In actual living experience with nature, however, cosmos is the All, which becomes man's house where he may enter-in-relation with the Absolute. *See* WORLD.

Creation (*Schöpfung*). Creation of the world as a divine act is a mystery, which Buber does not propose to unravel; neither does he accept the doctrine of "creation out of nothing." But out of this mystery comes the manifest participation of man in creation, not, to be sure, in the original divine act, but as he enters in dialogical relation with the world and its creator. Creation is manifest in every act of entering-in-relation, which renews itself constantly. "God's act of creation is speech; but the same is true of each lived moment" (I&W 16). As an original act, creation means bringing order out of chaos. In this respect man was created for the purpose of participating in the redemption of the world; this is his participation in creation.

Decision, To decide (*Entscheidung, sich entscheiden*). The ability to decide to follow the path of good is a factor in the act of entering-in-relation. It is the conscious motive power whereby evil is overcome by man. But this ability is manifest only in the encounter. "Only he who is aware of relation and knows the presence of Thou is capable of decision" (I&T

51). Indecision or lack of decision, which is evil, may come about either by refusing to enter-in-relation (wickedness) or by failure to do so, that is, by missing the moments of the encounter (sinfulness). Decision is thus conceived by Buber as a positive force that can give man direction or the way to good.

Destiny (*Schicksal*). Destiny is man's fulfilment of his category of being human which moves toward relation. It is not an outside force, such as fate, pushing him in this direction, but an inner constituent of his being human, as such. It therefore does not contradict freedom, as fate does; rather, "destiny and freedom are vowed unto each other" (I&T 53). *See* FATE.

Dialogue (*Dialog, Zwiesprache*). Dialogue means speech between two actual beings. It cannot take place when one speaks or thinks to himself, which is monologue. Neither is there dialogue when one speaks to a conceived other (*ein gedachter Andere*); it can occur only in an actual encounter with a living other, person with person. Even then, dialogue occurs only when one speaks with an other without holding oneself back, without premeditation, even as to the content of the conversation. The content flows in dialogue spontaneously through a genuine meeting with the other as a partner in speaking. The speaker's attention is turned unto the other as if he were the only one of concern at the moment. Through this "turning," dialogue gains its meaning as "the mutuality of inner action." Dialogue cannot be demanded. One is not ordered to respond; one is able to do it (BMM 8–10, 35).

Direction (*Richtung, Gerichtetsein*). Direction can only be a turning to God. When one turns away from

God, one lacks direction or has lost it. Direction is the good, as it is man's movement toward entering-in-relation. Absence of direction is confusion, chaos, indecision, disorientation (BMM 79).

Distance, Distancing (*Distanz, Distanzierung*). Distancing is one of the two primal movements (*Urdistanzierung*) between man and an other, in which man separates the other from himself as an object of experience and use. The second primal movement is entering-in-relation. This twofold movement is the principle of being human, the category *humanum* (KM 57). *See* RELATION.

Encounter, Confrontation (*Begegnung, das Gegenüber*). The meeting of man with an other is in the nature of an encounter, an unanticipated occurrence, a sudden happening, which calls for spontaneous response. Each encounter is unique, never repeated in the same form, even though one may meet the same other in many instances.

Escape. Escape from self-fulfilment occurs when man fails to realize his inborn Thou which strives to enter-in-relation with the other. He fails to meet the other in actuality, for he sees his inborn Thou as an object of his own *I*, or the world as an objectified *I*. This results in self-contradiction or alienation from the world. *See* INBORN THOU.

Evil (*Übel*). Basically, Buber considers evil as a lack or absence of direction, which is due either to man's refusal to respond to the other in the encounter or to his failure to do so. Man then lacks his wholeness as a human being. In the first instance the refusal is wickedness; in the second the failure is only sinfulness, that is, missing the moment when response is called for. Man is neither good nor evil, but has both good and evil inclinations. He may overcome his "evil inclination" by turning it into good, which is direction toward relation to God. To serve God with both inclinations is to serve Him with one's wholeness of being (KM 146; GE 95–97, 139).

Experience, Living Experience (*Erfahrung, Erlebnis*). In the German original, Buber distinguishes between *Erfahrung* and *Erlebnis*, which may be rendered into English as "experience" and "living experience," respectively. The first is applied to the I-It communication, in which man experiences an object mediated by sensation and through concepts as a thing of use, analysis, classification, etc. The second is applied to the I-Thou relation, in which there is an immediate living experience of an encounter with a being-as-a-whole, as subject with subject.

Faith (*Glaube*). Faith is not just a conviction or feeling of assurance that something exists, but rather a commitment to something. Faith in God means a trust that He is always present, "is there," when man is prepared to go forth to meet Him. The act of entering in relation with God's presence is an act of faith, which is one of the potencies of the human being. "The fundamental experience of faith itself should be regarded as the highest degree of the reality of meeting" (*Nachlese* 118, 123; I&W 29; BH 121, 126).

Fate (*Verhängnis*). Fate is a blind force outside of man which determines his life and conduct. In much of modern scientific thinking, laws of nature, represented as causal necessity, have assumed the character of fate, from which there is no escape. This is particularly true of the biologistic and historiosophical thinking which promulgates a belief in fate under disguise (I&T 57).

Freedom (*Freiheit*). Freedom has meaning only within the range of man's category of being human and of his role in creation and the redemption of the world. It is grounded in his power of decision to accept or reject this role. There is determination, which is purpose, in the divine act of creation, which manifests itself as a duality of I and Thou, though nothing further can be said about its origin. The free man recognizes this purpose and accepts his role as partner in it. He is free to enter-in-relation with the Thou and thus fulfil his destiny or to withdraw from the encounter. Man's freedom is thus to decide to act with the inclusive wholeness of his being and with full responsibility for the other and the absolute Thou. Freedom, in its positive sense, does not mean to be free from something or somebody (this is negative freedom), but rather to enter-in-relation with something. The very act of entering-in-relation *is* freedom (I&T 81–82; BMM 91–92; EG 68, 75–76).

Guilt (*Schuld*). When man is not there to respond to the call of the Thou, he is guilty, regardless of his feelings about it. Guilt is not to be identified with feeling; it is a state of being. Guilt is not in the human person but between him and the other whom he fails to meet. Guilt envelops man as an unfulfilled encounter, in which the human order of being has been violated (KM 132).

Image of God, Countenance (*Gestalt Gottes, Antlitz*). The word of God or revelation is actualized in personal and communal forms by converting it into objects of belief and cult. These are known as God's images or His Countenance. But in truth these are not images of God but of revelation in the world. Man never looks to God without the world. When he looks to them together, he forms God's Countenance, which is "a mixture of Thou and It," of the infinite and the finite (I&T 118).

Inborn Thou (*das eingeborene Du*). From the first moment of its life the child reaches out for contact with an other, first tactile and then visual, even before it becomes aware of an actual other. This is the *a priori* principle of relation, called the "inborn Thou." At first the child takes itself, its body, as the other, which manifests its striving for relation. As the child develops, its inborn Thou is realized through entering-in-relation with an actual other, that is, the child realizes its category *humanum*. The striving of the inborn Thou continues throughout life, for human relation never completes itself. This is manifest in man's striving for meeting with the Absolute Thou, as the complete act of relation (I&T 27–28).

Individual, The Singular, The Single One (*Individuum, der Einzige, der Einzelne*). Man is an individual in the sense that he is a unique, singular being (*der Einzige*) who is able to respond to fellowman and other beings on his own responsibility, as well as to distance himself from them. But this does not make the individual "the starting point or the goal of the human world." The latter view is that of the single one (*der Einzelne*). The individual has a place in the human world as a person, that is insofar as he and other persons form a community. Man, who is principally a being acting in a twofold way, "cannot be grasped in categories of the single one existing-for-itself, but in categories of his existing as man-with-man." "The single one is a fact of existence insofar as he steps into living relation with other single ones." Otherwise he is a mere abstraction (EG 127, 18; BMM 70, 203). *See* PERSON.

Individualism (*Individualismus*). This is the tendency of abstracting the individual as the single one existing-for-itself and making him the center of the human world. The opposite of individualism is collectivism, but actually the collective is conceived as an aggregate of individuals (*Einzelne*). "The time of individualism is past, despite efforts to revive it" (BMM 202).

Inertia (*Trägheit*). A privative state of the act of relation; a lack of decision to enter-in-relation. It is the condition in which man does not respond to the call of the Thou. "The roots of all evil persist in inertia" (I&W 18).

Inner Awareness (*Innewerden*). *See* OBSERVING.

Intuition. Generally, intuition is conceived as a human faculty capable of overcoming the duality which separates the observer from the observed or knowing from being. Buber does not recognize such a faculty, however, and rejects all theories of intuition which claim to have abolished this duality through a fusion of the knowing act with known reality. By intuition Buber means the state of man when his "whole being becomes one in the act of knowing," but the duality of observer and observed is not thereby eliminated. "Intuition binds us with the world against us . . . without being able to make us one with it. . . ." (PW 83, 86).

Love (*Liebe*). Love is one of the four potencies of the category of being human, as it manifests itself in interhuman relations. This is not to be taken merely as a feeling of love, that is, a psychological capacity. Feeling accompanies the potency of love as it does all other potencies, but love as such, as a potency, is an ontic act of man as a human being-as-a-whole.

"Feelings dwell *in* man, but man dwells in his love," which is between man and man (I&T 14).

Meaning of Life (*Sinn des Lebens*). The meaning of life, this life on earth, is not some fixed content to be transmitted in universal precepts, but must be confirmed by each one of us as we receive it when we go forth to meet the Absolute. This is revelation of the presence, which everyone is able to receive, but not as a one-time historical act, not as a tradition, but as a renewed living act of personal relation with God. "Everyone may confirm the received meaning only with the singleness of his being and the singleness of his life" (I&T 110, 111).

Meeting (*Begegnung*). Meeting is the act of being when it enters-in-relation with another being. "All real living is meeting," which is without mediation. (I&T 11).

Metacosmos. Metacosmos is a relation of the world to that which is not-world, that is, a primal duality. In its human form it manifests itself in the duality of man's twofold communication through the primary word-pairs I-Thou and I-It (I&T 101).

Mystery, Mysterium, Mysticism (*Geheimnis, Mysterium, Mystik*). Buber speaks of the mystery of certain origins of reality in the sense that they cannot be explained or even expressed in speech, as, for example, the mystery of the divine act of creation, or the mystery of the primal metacosmic duality. In the same sense he designates the hiddenness of God, out of which He reveals himself to man, as the great mysterium, which man cannot reach or grasp. But this is not to be confused with mysticism, which tries to overcome this limitation in order for man to know God and identify himself with Him. According to Buber, man can neither know nor be God (I&T 101; I&W 30–31). In the early stages of his philosophical development Buber went through what he called a "mystic" phase, but he abandoned it about the time of his publication of *Ich und Du* (in 1923) and in his subsequent writings (PW XV).

Object (*Gegenstand*). In the I-It communication man looks at an other as an object of observation, measurement, classification, and generally conceptual analysis. This is the mediated subject-object contact in which the knowing subject is distanced or separated from its object, as distinguished from the immediate subject-subject relation in I-Thou.

Objective Reality (*Wirklichkeit*). Objective reality is generally regarded as that which is outside the human subject. Since Buber recognizes only a twofold way of communication in which the subject (man) is always a participant, what does he mean by objective as differentiated from subjective? Objective reality, or the great "objectivum," as Buber calls it, can be only the relation of man with highest Thou, the Absolute. "Life in the Face [going out to meet God] is life in the One Reality, the only true 'objectivum'. . . ." (I&T 118).

Observing, Viewing, Inner Awareness (*Beobachten, Betrachten, Innewerden*). Speech may be expressed in three different forms, depending on how one "sees" the other: (1) by observing or noticing and recording every trait; (2) by viewing only the significant features of the other; (3) by an inner awareness that the other "says" something to me in my meeting him. The third form may be expressed by me in articulate or inarticulate speech or in silence. The first two forms are of the realm of I-It, the third of the I-Thou (BMM 8–10).

Ordered World *(geordnete Welt)*. *See* WORLD-ORDER.

Past *(Vergangenheit)*. The past in living human experience means the moment when man stepped out of the relational event and turned the Thou into an It, that is, an object of measurement in terms of a series of lapsed points of time or an ordered succession of time. Objects, therefore, are of the past, in contrast to the I-Thou of relation, which is present, where there is no awareness of time measurement. *See* TIME.

Place *(Ort)*. In living reality place is where man meets man, that is, the between of relation. " 'Between' is . . . the real place and bearer of what happens between man and man" (BMM 203). In the highest reality place is the locus where man realizes his destiny through "true folk-community," that is, the Center where communality stems from. What we may know of the long-awaited theophany is only its place, "and the place is called community" (BMM 7). *See* SPACE.

Person. Man who exists in mutuality with the other and confirms him is a person. The person lives *with* the world; the individual lives *in* the world. The person becomes conscious of himself as a participant in being, as *co*-existent and, thus, as a being, whereas the individual knows himself only as being thus. These are the two poles of humanity, which are manifest in each man as a twofold I (BMM 177–179). *See* INDIVIDUAL.

Potencies *(Potenzen)*. The potential ways of the act of communication between man and an other are four: cognition, art, love, and faith. They are not faculties of the psyche or of some part of the body, but potencies of the human category, in the sense that they are realizable in the acts of relating and distancing (KM 163).

Present, Presentness, Meeting (*Gegenwart, Vergegenwärtigung, Begegnung*). The German word *Gegenwart* conveys the full significance of present in the sense of an encounter with an other opposite (*gegen*) me. Similarly, the words *Vergegenwärtigung* and *Begegnung* (meeting), coming from the same root of *gegen* or opposite, convey the meaning of rendering present in the encounter. Present, thus, is not a temporal concept of arrested time, but sheer present, being there, at the moment of the meeting. Failure of meeting Buber calls *Vergegnung*. The other becomes present when I have an inner awareness of him, that is, as "personal making present" (KM 78).

Primary Words (*Grundworte*). These are not single words but word-pairs, I-Thou and I-It, which are primary acts of communication or speaking. They are not absolutes in themselves, not primary elements, but primary acts of communication which are manifest only in man's living experience, that is, as he speaks I-Thou or I-It and takes his stand in one or the other (I&T 3).

Reality (*Wirklichkeit*). Reality is not something given which may be described or explained in terms of objective facts. Reality occurs as man participates in the act of relation with others, without trying to appropriate them or to treat them as objects of use and calculation. Thus, the I is made real to the extent that participation is made complete. Reality is not in the I or the It, nor in the Thou, each in itself, but between I and Thou. Man knows reality by being there when it occurs between him and other beings. When Buber speaks of "the crisis of the between," he has in mind the crisis of reality (BMM 125, 205; I&T 136–137); *Wirklichkeit* is also translated as "actuality".

Redemption (*Erlösung*). The whole of man together with the whole of the world, not just the human soul, is to be redeemed. God wants man and the world to be redeemed, as the completion of creation. Man's role in redemption is to respond with unreserved responsibility to the call of the eternal Thou. God's call to man is revelation, as His call to the world is creation. Man's response, his turning and return, is redemption as seen from the human side. Man as a whole, with his spirit, body, and soul, including both of his inclinations, is to be redeemed. Redemption is not from evil, but the redeeming of evil (I&W 37).

Relation (*Beziehung*). Relation is the spiritual tie that comes into existence when I-Thou is spoken. The other primal act is experience, which belongs to the realm of I-It. In the German original this distinction is expressed by the terms *Beziehung* and *Erfahrung*, respectively (*Das dialogische Prinzip*, 9–10).

Response, Responsibility (*Antwort, Verantwortung*). Response is the act of turning to the other and confirming him as a Thou, and not using him as an It. Man may turn toward or away from the other, that is, respond or refuse or fail to respond. True response can come only with full responsibility for the other who is entrusted to me. Man's responsibility is a response to the divine call. (BMM 61, 92).

Return (*Umkehr*). When man goes astray from the way of God, he can return by deciding to resume direction to Him. Return does not mean going back to an innocent, sinless beginning, but signifies a decision to go forth again on the way to meeting God.

Return can come only as a turning, making a complete swing away from waywardness and toward God, Who also turns to man as the latter returns (I&W 19–21).

Revelation (*Offenbarung*). Revelation is God's call to man to participate in redemption of the world. What is revealed or given to man is his responsibility, and his turning signifies his acceptance of it. Not a content is revealed but a present, as a power which assures mutuality and confirms the meaning of life on earth (I&T 110–111; I&W 27).

Space (*Raum*). As a measurable quantity space may be conceived as the distance between objects or as the overall continuum in which objects appear and may be measured. In this physical sense, space means extension, limit, and duration. But in the realm of I-Thou space signifies exclusiveness as well as endurance. When we speak of a Thou appearing in space, we mean that it is an independent, exclusive being that endures in confrontation with the I. Everything else is not its limit but a background (I&T 30–31).

Speech, Speaking (*Sprache, reden*). Speech or speaking in the I-Thou relation is an act of turning to the other, even when nothing is said in words. But speech in I-It is a turning away from the other. Both are primary acts. Speaking means addressing oneself to an other. In essence, speech is dialogical; one does not truly speak to oneself. Speech is not in man, but man lives in speech, which is between man and man (BMM 199; KM 106, 117–118).

Spirit (*Geist*). Spirit is not a substance or special kind of being and not a human faculty, but a between which comes into being in the ontic act of I-Thou relation between man and that which is not-world. Spirit is thus not in man or outside of him, but man lives in spirit when he enters-in-relation. Spirit is objectified when the Thou is turned into It, but it will not lose its force as long as man continues to strive for relation and turns again and again to the eternal Thou (BMM 191; PW 187).

Spirituality (*Geistigkeit*). Spirit becomes degraded into spirituality when man, instead of going forth to meet with God, tries to take hold of Him for self-gratification. This is true of all relations when the Thou is turned into an object of self-satisfaction only. By separating a "spiritual life" from our actual daily affairs we create a make-believe spirituality, devoid of any power to influence our lives (I&T 50–51).

Subject, Subjectivity (*Subjekt, Subjektivität*). Buber designates the I as subject when the not-I is an It, and as subjectivity when the not-I is a Thou. The first is identified as individual; the second, as person (I&T 63).

The I (*das Ich*). The I exists only insofar as an actual living being says I-Thou or I-It. "Becoming *I*, I speak Thou" and "Through the Thou a man becomes *I*" (I&T 11, 28). The I, taken by itself, that is outside these word-pairs, is only an abstraction that may be analyzed in psychology, sociology, or some anthropological science, but may not be grasped as a living being-as-a-whole. In this respect, "the word *I* is the true shibboleth of mankind" (I&T 65). Spoken in truth, the *I* in I-Thou is not the same as the *I* in I-It. What is the same is man-as-a-whole, who speaks one or the other word-pair and takes his stand either in relation or in distance. Inasmuch as the I enters reality through speaking, Buber designates the state which is prior to the I's becoming as *vorichhaft*, and the state that follows as *nachichhaft*. The I, as such, he calls *Ichhaftigkeit* (I&T 22–23).

The It (*das Es*). *It* has existence only as connected with the I in the word-pair I-It. The term It signifies an object of observation, classification, thinking, using, but never an actual being-as-a-whole. The It may thus be given objective, relative existence only as an abstraction from the living experience of man with nature. The It may be a single fact of observation or a complex scientific construct, even the universe constructed as an objective totality. The It may be the same in many observations as long as it is consistently constructed out of the same facts or elements, according to a theory free from self-contradiction. The It falls apart, becomes nonexistent, the moment it appears to be self-contradictory.

The Thou (*das Du*). The *Thou* is the other which is encountered by man in the I-Thou relation. As a being-as-a-whole, it exists in actuality, independently of the I, yet as a Thou it has meaning only in the I-Thou relation. The term Thou signifies that it is being addressed by the I and is thus not another I in the relation. As a being-as-a-whole it may also be an I when it addresses an other as its Thou. Although the other may be the same being throughout, it manifests different forms in each new encounter as a new I-Thou, since no encounter repeats itself in the same form. *See also* ABSOLUTE THOU.

The Way (*der Weg*). The ever renewed moments of going forth to meet the eternal Thou are the way to God. Although man may step in and out of the way, it is the real continuum of his world insofar as he builds it through constantly turning and returning to

way is "the course and countercourse of
al and eternally present Word in history"
9).

it). In the realm of I-It, time is a measurable
of points in succession, dealing with a lapsed
er of events or objects in space. In the realm of
hou, time means bounded moments of entering-in-
relation. It is the living moment of purely intensive
dimension. There is no series of succession, for each
act of relation is unique and nonrepetitive. Historical time is the moment ripe for revelation, when man
is ready to meet with the eternal Thou, or the finite
with the infinite. Such moments, too, are not repeti-
tive in the same form; each is a unique occurrence
when man goes forth to meet God (I&T 30, 117).

Turning (*Kehre, Wendung, sich hinwenden*). Turning
is manifest in man's addressing the other as Thou.
Speaking, in truth, is turning to the other without
holding oneself back. Turning may also come as a
turning point in man's wayward conduct when he
decides to return to the way of God. "The turning
is not a return to an earlier 'sinless' state," but an
act of mutuality at any stage of civilization. In its
primal sense, turning is addressing or speaking with
another as Thou. It is a turning of one's very existence when one is in crisis. "The power of turning
that radically changes the situation, never reveals
itself outside the crisis" (PW 237; BMM 22; I&W
245).

World, Our World, Real World (*Welt, unsere Welt,
wirkliche Welt*). The world as an entity, a wholeness, a unity, is a concept formed when man distances himself from everything not-himself. He then
posits a separate world which stands over against him.

But in and by itself such a world un
conceived by man without his other pri
ment of entering-in-relation. The world
man being human, that is, with his two
munication. The world is thus a human w
may be spoken of as "our world." But this
make it a subjective world. It is rather a c
through the twofold movement of man in his
experience with nature. The "real world" is tl
which comes into being through man's relation
the Absolute. In all cases, for Buber the world
this world of our life on earth (BMM 61-6
60-62).

World-Order, Ordered World (*Weltordnung,* g
Welt). The world in which man participa
partner in creation is a purposive world-o
Thou relations. It has its own time, space, a
but not in the same sense as in the ordered
I-It. In the world-order space is exclusiveness, time
is the living moment of relation, cause is mutuality.
The ordered world is posited and constructed out of
temporal and spatial elements in causal interaction.
It is measurable, calculable in a spatiotemporal frame
of reference, such as mathematico-physical coordinates (I&T 31-33, 115).

NOTES

NOTES